A TASTE OF
WARTIME BRITAIN

edited by
NICHOLAS WEBLEY

ROgOOD

First published by Thorogood Publishing Ltd 2003
Reprinted 2004

Thorogood Publishing Ltd
10-12 Rivington Street
London EC2A 3DU

Telephone: 020 7749 4748
Fax: 020 7729 6110
Email: info@thorogood.ws
Web: www.thorogood.ws

A CIP catalogue record for this book is available from
the British Library.

ISBN 1 85418 213 7

Printed in India by Replika Press

Designed by Driftdesign

For Patricia MacMillan with love

THE
BRITISH NAVY
guards the freedom of us all

PROTECTING THE
'SALTWATER HIGHWAYS'

COPYRIGHT DISCLAIMER

Foreword by David Croft OBE

Co-writer and producer of BBC's classic comedy series Dad's Army

 The book revives so many memories for me. I was there. At the age of just 17 during the evacuation I was a volunteer Billeting Officer in Poole, Dorset. Life was full of laughs and tears. Troubled housewives who had given homes to evacuees from London came to us with their problems and didn't think it quite right to ask someone so young for rubber sheets for kids who wet the bed.

On my 18th birthday I watched the Battle of Britain from Primrose Hill and witnessed the Spitfires and Hurricanes buzzing around the Heinkels and Dorniers, cheering when the Nazis were shot down, like present day 18 year olds watching a goal scored at football. Two nights later I was knocked off my perch on the downstairs sofa as the next door house took a direct hit.

As an Air Raid Warden I organised fire watching rotas, made a collection to buy a stirrup pump and helped worried old ladies into their gas masks.

As an actor I went up to Bangor in North Wales where the BBC Variety Department took over all the Church halls as studios to keep the programmes going and commandeered every bed and breakfast to house the actors, producers and musicians.

As a soldier I dodged the V1 bombs and as a young officer I was blown out of bed by a supersonic V2 rocket which landed near Hyde Park Corner. I heard it arrive after it exploded.

The wonderful true stories in *A Taste of Wartime Britain* bring all the memories flooding back. Nicholas Webley has compiled a fine book. Read it – and don't let it all happen again.

Acknowledgments

I am grateful for the help of the following in the production of this book, in particular those who gave me their stories for the 'They Were There' pieces – I wasn't, so it would have been a thin book without them – their names are appended to the relevant contributions. I hope they forgive me for taking up so much of their time over the years.

My gratitude to Angela, Catherine, Neill and all at Thorogood. My thanks also to: Rob Blann at www.yourmemories.co.uk for 'Monkhouse in the doghouse' and making me laugh out loud. David Croft OBE. The United States National Archive cannot be thanked enough for their tireless assistance, expertise and professionalism. Steven Spielberg and all the people at DreamWorks for helping to bring this book to the bookstands. HOLNET (www.holnet.org.uk) is a project developed by the Worshipful Company of Information Technologists with funding from the Sir John Cass Foundation and with material provided by the Imperial War Museum. Their more than generous assistance and generosity has been invaluable – in particular for that on the section relating to the Blitz. Willard Reese and the 457th Bomb Group for their invaluable help and for their tireless work in recording the events of WW2. I recommend their site to any who wish to know more: www.457thbombgroup.org. The George B. Gosney photograph collection (courtesy of 'Moofy'). To Wayne and Darren Wilkins at www.homesweethomefront.co.uk – they deserve a medal. To the website www.transdiffusion.org and Dafydd Hancock in particular for his excellent contribution 'Forces of Light' copyright Dafydd Hancock.

To the anonymous person who sent me a collection of photographs and cuttings, that had been collected by his grandfather, to 'put to good use so no one forgets'. Thank you whoever you are and I hope you get the chance to see the result of your grandfather's foresight – he was one heck of a collector – and your generosity.

To all who have taken the time to record their memories, in so many forms, of WW2. I hope this book has done justice to your dedication.

To 'Betty' for bothering, all those years ago, to write down her recipes and thoughts which set me on course to write this book.

WAR INSPIRED COMRADESHIP

Contents

Part three
RECIPES FROM THE
HOME FRONT

Introduction

Writing the introduction to this book has turned out to be the most difficult job I could have tackled, after reading the sheer quality of the contributions from those who have given so generously of their time to this project. Therefore the best thing I can do is to write what I feel will be the closest I can get to living up to them.

Many books have been written about the Second World War, in any one year close on a thousand books are published, a mere fraction of those actually written, on the subject. My aim with *A Taste of Wartime Britain* is to tell the stories of those who would not normally get their words into print and give some background information on life at that time. In sleeve notes for my last book, to which I refer on occasions, *Betty's Wartime Diary 1939 – 1945*, David Croft OBE – co-creator of the BBC classic comedy series 'Dad's Army' – said that ordinary people seldom write books as they are usually too busy 'doing' for others. In this I have in a small way set out to redress the balance about a period I find one of the most fascinating, and pivotal, in the history of the British Isles and Western Europe.

I have included some stories that do not necessarily relate to Britain; this is simply because they are of such interest and value that I could not leave them out – that of George Parnell being one.

I am most appreciative of all those who have been so helpful on this project. Set down in this one volume is an attempt to communicate some idea of what it was like to live day-to-day under the appalling shadow of war.

Social history can be studied in many ways. One can read learned works by the shakers and movers in government and the military, but for the fine weave of life I advocate scrutiny of popular culture contemporary with the times and talking to those who were there and, if possible, recording what they have to tell you.

It would have been impossible to include stories that parallel everyone's experiences of WW2, but I hope that those I have will give a new slant to already held ideas.

The victors write history it is said. Rarely is it written by the ordinary people who held everything together when all around them was just falling to pieces, such as during the Blitz. There will be gaps left; it has not been possible to interview a representative from all walks of life, or from all parts of Britain. Unlike earlier times, however, it is possible now to compensate for this shortfall. I have therefore thought of *A Taste of Wartime Britain* as not just a book, but also a 'portal', opening on to other times. To that end I have given Website addresses that will be of endless interest to readers with the desire to learn more; unlike the written word the new technologies offer the chance for immediate input and constant development. The first part of this book is intended to set the stories of the second part into context. The second part is the result of much time and travel 'downloading' the memories of the people who were witness to war on a day-to-day basis. They are not set down in any particular order as the stories overlap timeframes, so to have done it that way would have been pointless. Part three is a selection of recipes that were part of *Betty's Wartime Diary 1939-1945* – published in 2002 – and give an idea of what it was like to try to feed family and friends, and pets, from such meagre rations as available at that time.

I admit to being a softie. I cannot really even begin to truly understand the hardships and sacrifice made that gave me the freedom to be soft and the kind of person who finds it hard to get up in the morning and moans if the weather is bad. I wasn't there to witness the truly dreadful events that so many did. For that I am grateful.

It is said by historians that The Romans were so successful in conquering because 'they were better at sticking bits of metal into their enemy than anyone else'. Today success depends upon the 'beauty' of the weapons and how many they can kill with minimal risk to the user.

I remember what one American serviceman, currently serving, said to me: 'Nobody likes doing what it is we are trained to do, but someone has to know how.' As recent events have proved it is not an option to drop our guard against those who wish to oppress others by the use of violence. It is necessary to be in a position to show those who may harbour expansionist ambitions – be they territorial or ideological – that it is not worth their while; that they can and will be stopped and brought to book. The situation in Bosnia of the early nineties is a recent case that proves what can happen if positive steps are not taken at an early stage. Because of dithering, when Serbian ambitions were becoming evident, it was necessary for a full-scale war to be waged – and a hard lesson learned.

As populations grow, and living space and resources are more and more stretched, there is potential for even more conflict. From the first time Homo erectus coveted his neighbour's dinner, and bashed him on the head with a stick to get it, there has been the temptation to take by force what is not given freely. It would seem from the testament of history that things have changed little.

The time has come to find a better way to solve problems I think. War must always be the last resort but the aggressor given no quarter lest he think his ambition will not be resisted and the desire for peace mistaken for a sign of weakness, not of reason. If history teaches anything it is this:

'War Is Hell', but sometimes unavoidable.

Nicholas Webley

Part One
THE PRELUDE TO WAR

'Potato Pete'

Part One
THE PRELUDE TO WAR

Europe of the 1930s was in turmoil and London, along with the rest of Britain, was preparing for war.

In World War I there had been two major raids on London in the summer of 1917, made by Zeppelin bombers. By 1939, air technology had developed rapidly. The notion of new and improved planes and bombs, capable of even greater destruction directed at London filled people with foreboding. It was clear that the authorities were going to have to prepare themselves for attacks on civilians.

Air-raid precautions to protect the people of London were made compulsory by the government as early as 1937. In April of that year an Air Raid Warden service was set up. Just over a year later 200,000 people had been recruited into that service.

The fear of poison gas attacks was another threat to Londoners. Poison gas had been used in the First World War on the Western Front. Consequently, gas masks were provided for all and it was made compulsory to carry them at all times.

Londoners began to build a picture in their minds of what a war would mean for them, how it would affect them in their very homes.

PHONEY WARTIME

At 11:15am on Sunday 3rd September 1939, on BBC radio, the Prime Minister, Neville Chamberlain, announced the declaration of war on Nazi Germany. At 11:27am the air-raid warning sirens wailed throughout London. Londoners had experienced practice bomb alerts before but this one must have felt different, more real perhaps, as the people filed into the shelters guided by police and ARP Wardens.

Thus began the period known as the 'Phoney War'. No bombs fell that day. Why this postponement of hostilities? Why was London not being pounded with thousands of tons of high-explosive and incendiary bombs? Had Germany forgotten how effective in cracking morale the destruction of cities could be? The answer lay in the practicalities of war. Germany at that time simply did not have the systems in place to mount an effective, planned bombing campaign of the magnitude desired. They had plans on the drawing board for a heavy bomber – the Heinkel He-177. It had, however, not been found to be up to the job.

All this meant, without wishing to go into the arcane details of the situation, that when Goering began his bombing of Britain it was with an inadequate infrastructure and inferior equipment to that desired. Also when the night-bombing campaign commenced it was with crews woefully under-trained for such a task.

Hitler had intended to leave London untouched; harbouring the desire to occupy the city intact; the Fuhrer had forbidden any attacks on London. There were plans and ruses in the background for the time when Britain would capitulate and many among the British establishment favoured this option. Some would have been the puppets of the Nazis. Members of the Royal Family included, along with some aristocratic families sympathetic to the Fascist cause. It is an uncomfortable thought, even more than sixty years after WW2, that there are still more than a few diamond studded swastika brooches and pins in the jewellery boxes of some aristocratic families. Unpalatable details but, be assured, factual. Some of these potential sympathisers are around today and occasionally are called upon to pontificate on certain things. In less enlightened countries they would not have made it into the 1950s let alone the 21st Century.

Therefore the initial German bombing campaign was intended only to render the British air defences impotent. Hitler needed air-superiority in order for his 'Operation Sealion' – the invasion of Britain – to succeed.

But war is a strange and unpredictable beast. On August 24th 1940 two flights of bombers, whose target was the oil refineries at Thames Haven, missed their objective – reasons given vary, it is enough to say that the bombs fell indiscriminately across London. A very bad move on the part of those responsible. The ramifications were massive for both sides of the conflict.

Churchill ordered retaliatory strikes against Berlin on August 25th and 26th. Eighty-one Wellingtons, Hampdens and Whitleys were sent to do the job. Although this was, relatively, an insignificant raid it infuriated Hitler. The British bombers returned four times in the following ten nights. Thus was the die cast. Hitler, having been persuaded by Field Marshall Albrecht Kesselring and Commander-in-Chief of the Air Force Hermann Goering, agreed that London was from that time not to be considered a no go area for German bombers; no longer was what the Nazi's considered the beating heart of European resistance the 'Forbidden Target'. It has been argued that this was the very moment when Germany lost control of the air campaign. This subject alone is worth additional study.

On Saturday, September 7th 1940, at 4.00pm, three hundred and twenty bombers, protected by 600 fighters, flew over the coastline of Kent. It was everything Kesselring could get to fly, and head for London.

THE CITY THAT WOULD NOT DIE

Hitler added many words to the lexicon of terror and abominable deeds. 'Blitzkrieg', meaning 'Lightning War', being one of them. London, between 7th September 1940 and 11th May 1941, was bombed and bombed and bombed. Seventy nights of bombing. It is difficult for those who have lived in times of relative peace to comprehend the full horror of what that means. The uncertainty of it all. Not knowing if those you loved would see another day. Whether you would see another day. To feel 'lucky' if you merely lost your home, everything you owned but kept your life. It was horror on a scale not known in these islands before. Of course Germany did indeed reap the whirlwind promised by Arthur 'Bomber' Harris that day on a roof in London. That, as the saying goes, is another story. This, however, is the story of how a city defied the barbarian because its inhabitants did not know the meaning of the word defeat.

In the days when this book is being written the word 'loss' means something different to what it did in the war. Every day we are implored to litigate if we trip over an uneven paving stone by the 'no win no fee' culture. How would most of us cope today if we lost all in one night of burning, unstoppable hell? If all we had lay ruined and smoking? We would most likely call our lawyer, see who we could sue. Not in WW2 however. Those who survived a night of bombing dusted off and went to work. Clambering over the rubble and broken glass.

THE FIRST RAID ON LONDON

So it was that the first bombers arrived to drop incendiary bombs on the London docks; 348 bombers with an escort of 617 fighters made up that first attack. Incendiary bombs were used to start fires and it was the light of the docks aflame that guided the other bombers to their target. That first attack had to be endured until about 6.00pm. Night was to afford no cover for two hours later, guided by the lights of the fires already burning, a second wave of bombers loomed over the horizon. In this way, bombing continued relentlessly all through the night until 4.30 the next morning. Here are the memories of Arthur who was witness to that first raid:

'It was Saturday afternoon. My dad had given me and my brother some wood and paper to make some kites with. We were having some trouble getting hold of any string, but managed to scrounge some off a mate of ours in exchange for half a bar of chocolate. We were in our back yard when we heard the planes coming over. Then we heard a sort of 'woooooooof' noise. I don't remember it as a bang or an explosion. It was loud enough to bring mum and dad outside. We all ran out into the street and could see the clouds of smoke rising from the

docks. It was a funny old sight. We were all pretty frightened when we realised that it was bombs being dropped. It went on for ages and we all went into the Anderson shelter. My dad and uncle had put the shelter in months before and there were benches to sit and sleep on. Not much else though. When the bombs stopped we came out and had a look around after about half an hour. It was very quiet. I remember I was so scared that I could hear the blood pumping in my ears. My mum looked very sad and I remember hearing her whispering to my dad how scared she was. Then the Germans came back and bombed again until the morning. We all spent the night in the shelter, even the cat. I hated the Germans for frightening us all that day and I am sad to say I hate them still, and I always will. I cheered later in the war when I heard how hard we had bombed Berlin, Hamburg and Dresden. The Germans robbed me and my brother of a proper childhood and split my family up forever, so I think they deserve all the hate.'

This was the start of the Blitz.

The Blitz fell upon all of London: shops, offices, churches, factories, docks and suburban homes all found themselves victims. It was nine months before Londoners were able to enjoy a full night's sleep, free of air-raids, free of sirens, free of the screaming shattering sound of bombs falling around them.

CLEARING UP AFTER A RAID

SOUNDS OF THE BLITZ

One historian, who lived through it, describes the noises of the Blitz:

'First, there was the alert, a wail rising and falling for two minutes. There was not one siren but a series, as the note was taken up by borough after borough. Then, there was a heavy, uneven throb of the bombers. Then there were many noises. The howling of dogs; the sound of high explosive bombs falling, like a tearing sheet; the clatter of little incendiaries on the roofs and pavements; the dull thud of walls collapsing; the burglar alarms which destruction had set ringing; the crackle of flames, a relishing, licking noise, and the bells of the fire engines'.

ANGUS CALDER 'THE PEOPLE'S WAR' P196

AFTER A RAID NOWHERE WHICH HAD BEEN BOMBED WAS SAFE

THE SECOND GREAT FIRE OF LONDON

On December 29th 1940 came one of the heaviest, if not the heaviest, raid on London since September. The accepted wisdom of the day was that it had been Hitler's intention to set London ablaze, to cause the 'Second Great Fire of London', as the prelude to an invasion in the New Year. Because of other commitments protecting the ports there were no night fighters over London on that terrible night. However, soon after 10.00pm the German high command sent orders for all aircraft, then engaged, to return to their bases immediately as the weather was deteriorating and fog was closing in around the German aerodromes. 'General Weather' was the saviour of the Nation's capital that night. There is little doubt from the records that this raid was intended to have been the fiercest of the war. During the three hour raid, according to the *Daily Mail* of Monday December 31st 1940, ten thousand incendiary devices were dropped on the capital.

GAS WAS GENUINELY FEARED BUT NEVER USED

CASUALTIES OF THE BLITZ

First night: 7th/8th September 1940	430 killed
	16,000 seriously injured
From 7th September 1940 to New Year's Day 1941	13,339 killed
	17,937 seriously injured.
Night of May 10th/11th 1941	1,436 killed
	1,752 seriously injured

On 29th December 1940, 275 years after the Great Fire of London, a two-hour German attack started 1,500 fires throughout London. The Fire Brigade and the Auxiliary Fire Services worked around the clock. As many as 100 million gallons of water were used in a period of just 24 hours in an attempt to extinguish the uncontrollable fires, around 1,400 of these in the centre of the city itself. Although few people lived there, the firestorm still resulted in 163 deaths and widespread damage was done to offices and shops in the centre of London.

Britain took a most horrific revenge for the second Fire of London in 1945 when it created a terrifying night of fire in the German city of Dresden. It is thought that as many as 135,000 German civilians could have been killed in those fires.

A DIRECT HIT CAUSES CHAOS

LONDON SHELTER CENSUS

The anvil upon which the Nazi hammer fell most was of course London. These details make fascinating reading and go some way to give a flavour of how Londoner's lived.

In November 1940 the government took a Shelter Census of central London to see who was sheltering where. It found:

- 4% were sheltering in the Underground system

- 9% in public shelters

- 27% in domestic shelters [Anderson and Morrison shelters]

- Most Londoners stayed in their homes, sleeping downstairs, under stairs, under tables, in cupboards. If they used a shelter at home then it would have been either an Anderson or a Morrison shelter.

HOME FROM HOME FOR MANY

RATIONING AND WHAT IT MEANT

WEEKLY ALLOWANCE

An example of an adults weekly food ration allowance in 1943 was:

- 3 pints of milk
- 3 1/4lb – 1lb meat
- 1 egg or 1 packet of dried eggs every 2 months
- 3-4oz cheese
- 4oz bacon and ham
- 2oz tea
- 8oz sugar
- 2oz butter
- 2oz cooking fat
- + 16 points a month for other rationed foods (usually tinned) subject to availability.

These weekly rations were stretched with the help of un-rationed extras like bread (incidentally not rationed until after the war), cereal, potatoes, offal and fruit and vegetables.

EVACUATION

With war imminent, the Government ordered plans to evacuate children (and others) from London and other cities into effect on the 1st September 1939. The Government estimated that 3,500,000 people would be evacuated in this period alone. In fact in the first four days of September 1939 1,500,000 people took up the offer to evacuate to safer areas away from the major towns. Many people preferred to stay at home and take their chances rather than saying goodbye to their loved ones.

However, the threat of heavy bombings and poison gas was real in September 1939. Newsreels reported a new form of warfare that Poland had witnessed called the Blitzkrieg which Britain did not feel prepared for. The Government knew that the country was nowhere near ready for war but all was done, that could be, to rectify this. The Local Defence Volunteers (LDV) was formed to prepare for the Hun invading Britain and although in real terms the LDV was no match for an invading German army, symbolically the LDV was a giant in raising Britain's morale. However, fears of a Blitzkrieg soon turned to more of a Sitzkrieg.

The following figures give an idea of the number of people at this time leaving the major cities to safer havens.

Mothers and Children	350,000 to 400,000
Unaccompanied Children	141,000
Expectant Mothers	20,700
Total	**1,250,000**

It must be remembered that evacuation did save countless lives and was necessary to protect the vulnerable. Try asking yourself the question 'What would you have done?'

It is a dilemma that thankfully most of us have never had to face.

THE AMERICAN AIRFORCE ENTERTAIN

FORCES OF LIGHT

It is well known that World War II was the making of the BBC. The pre-war BBC had been easily accused of being staid and overly educative, not least by Associated-British Picture Corporation's film 'Radio Parade of 1935' satirising the BBC as the 'NBG' and deriding its experiments in television and dull programming.

The original radio service had early on been divided into the National Programme and the Regional Programme, turning the disadvantages of attempting complete coverage of a geographically varied country using medium and long wave transmissions. The Regional Programme, which despite its name retained a London-based feel in many ways as soon as networking of the transmitters became practical, was home to news programmes, features and talks. The

National Programme was the base from which news, features and talks were also distributed, but with music, drama and variety making more of an appearance than on the Regional.

Before the first siren had sounded over London, the BBC reacted with what now looks like panic to the situation in Poland but was then the only sensible action. It closed the Regional and the National took its frequencies, taking the name 'Home Service', though this was officially a 'merger' of the two services into one networked station.

Practically, this could not last. The population of the UK were suddenly left with their cinemas closed 'for the duration', their sports fixtures abandoned, curfews on pubs and nightclubs and a limit on capacity for such diverse entertainments as dance halls and museums. Death from the skies was expected – boredom was the reality.

On 7th January 1940 the former home of the National – 5XX from Daventry on 1500 metres supplemented by local fillers – was given over to a new station, the Forces Programme. In reality, this was a lighter version of the old National, with the BBC taking the excuse of 'officially' serving the Forces only to provide a service it could not have brought itself to consider a year before.

The Forces instantly became the most popular service in the United Kingdom, and amongst English-speakers in soon-to-be Occupied Europe. Its mixture of drama, comedy, popular music, features, quiz shows and variety was richer and more varied than the National, ostensibly designed to cheer and console lonely servicemen in the UK and beyond.

The phenomenal success of the Forces Programme was nothing, however, to the effect that its replacement would have.

With the build-up toward D-Day and the Normandy landings, the British Isles began to fill up with American servicemen. Even those from the Middle West of the US – hometown boys with little or no experience of the wider world – found the UK to be dull. The people were poor, hungry and threadbare after almost five years of total war. The beer was dire, the sausages inedible, the sport absent or just plain odd, the music almost a decade out of date and the blackout caused more trouble than the excitement that may have been expected.

In reaction to this, the BBC took the bold step of abolishing the Forces Programme. In its place began, on 27th February 1944, the General Forces Programme. This new station retained the most popular features of the old Forces network, but replaced some of the, shall we say, less populist features of the network with material that was for the times relentlessly popular.

More comedy, drama and variety stars were imported from the States – and most importantly the style of presentation and speed of action so noticeable in American commercial network radio made its first appearance in the UK. The British population – already largely hooked on the strapping American rescuers – were enamoured and impressed by the new 'Americanised' service. Hungry for genuine entertainment when the economic and social situation was at its lowest, the GFP provided a steady diet of popularism that is still remembered fondly by that generation today.

When the final all-clear sounded, the American forces in the UK began to immediately drain away. The factory workers – mostly women by this point – began to return home to produce the generation that now holds political power both here and in the US. Yet the GFP continued. It provided a valuable service while Britain began the slow crawl back to normality.

But its raison d'être – the General Forces themselves – also disappeared from the barrack rooms and mess halls across northern Europe, demobbed back to the homes, lives and jobs they had missed for many long years. The BBC announced its new pattern of broadcasting not too long after VE-Day. The Home Service, using the former Regional Programme transmitters, would itself be regionalised back to the approximate pre-war boundaries with a middle-class mandate. The GFP's frequency would revert to the National Programme – but this would tellingly be renamed the Light Programme. A third network would be born to take the highly educated listeners away from the Light and the Home. The Television Service was to be relaunched from Ally Pally.

The Light Programme began on 29th July 1945, aimed at a specifically domestic audience. The GFP began to fade away before finally expiring on 31st December 1946. But the Light Programme born from the GFP had something that the former National Programme did not – the experience of those war years, Americanised popular entertainment styles and an ethos of presentation far removed from Reith's original plans. WW2 was the making of the BBC reputation. And the General Forces Programme was the making of the BBC's longevity.

BROADCASTING HOUSE

THE LEGEND THAT IS THE 'HOME GUARD'

Most of us have, at sometime or other, enjoyed the BBC television series 'Dad's Army', with its somewhat light-hearted look at the Second World War's Home Guard. With its memorable signature tune 'Who do you think you are kidding Mr Hitler?' it's usually among the first imagery evoked when thinking of the Home Guard.

However, despite this portrayal, in its time the Home Guard represented a formidable force of willing volunteers ready to give up their lives in protection of their country. Indeed, should Hitler's Germany have succeeded with its invasion plans, the Home Guard were ready and waiting.

So how did it all begin and how did the Home Guard hope to protect Britain from a seemingly unstoppable Germany?

This is a brief history of the Home Guard.

INVASION FEARS AND THE LDV

It was with considerable haste during the spring of 1940, that Britain began to prepare itself for a potential German invasion. With the government all too aware of how real this threat was becoming and how it was affecting Britain's morale, it began to think up ways of how the country could be helped should the unthinkable ever happen.

Many citizen's felt that they wanted to do their bit, even though they may have been seen as too old, or too young, to be in uniform. This desire to serve led to the newly-appointed Secretary of State for War, Anthony Eden, to make the following speech. No one could have predicted the enthusiasm with which this opportunity to serve was taken up: an unbelievable 250,000 signed up to be Local Defence Volunteers (LDVs) within the first 24 hours.

EDEN'S HOME GUARD SPEECH

May 14th 1940, 9.00pm

'Since the war began the Government has received countless inquiries from all over the kingdom from men of all ages who are, for one reason or another, not at present engaged in military service, and who wish to do something for the defence of their country. Well, now is your opportunity. We want large numbers of such men in Great Britain, who are British subjects, between the ages of 17 and 65... to come forward now and offer their services.... The name of the new Force which is now to be raised will be 'The Local Defence Volunteers'... This name describes its duties in three words.... This is a part-time job, so that there will be no need for any volunteer to abandon his present occupation.... When on duty you will form part of the armed forces.... You will not be paid, but you will receive a uniform and will be armed...'

Thus, in that succinct broadcast a legend, a true legend, was born. The men who signed up for the LDV (later of course to be renamed the Home Guard), were brave individuals; had the British Isles been invaded the men of the Home Guard would have had a most difficult and dangerous time. The very act of volunteering was in itself a sign of true bravery.

In the speech he warned of the threat of invasion by means of German parachute regiments and how this awful scenario would need an established fighting force already in place to see off these unwanted visitors. He urged all male civilians aged 17-65* who had (for whatever reason) not been drafted into the services, to put themselves forward for the sake of their country and help to form a new fighting force called 'The Local Defence Volunteers' or LDV for short, or (as some people later joked), 'Look, Duck and Vanish'!

Eden had made clear in his broadcast that the passing of a medical examination wouldn't be necessary and that providing you were male, capable of free movement and of the right age, all one needed to do was enrol at their local police station.

It's true to say that if Eden was ever in any doubt about the impetus his broadcast had had on the general public, his fears were soon to be allayed. For, by the end of the following day, some 250,000 men had volunteered, with these volunteers coming from all walks of life including mining, factory working, public transport and farming to note but a few. By the end of the month a total of 750,000 men had come forward. Some problems did exist initially with many police stations soon running out of the enrolment forms. However, despite this small inconvenience it was good to see that Britain shared in the government's view that it had to guard itself in some manner and 'better be safe than sorry'!

LDV UNIFORM AND ARMS

The early LDV uniforms were scarce, but those available consisted quite simply of a denim battledress and armband proudly displaying the LDV initials. Willing volunteers of the Women's Voluntary Service (WVS) were among those who made these LDV armbands.

A CHANGE OF NAME

In a moment of inspiration Winston Churchill renamed the LDV the Home Guard, although later it became affectionately known quite simply as 'Dad's Army'. Considering the LDV had only been in operation for a month and a half at the time of this announcement, it came as a surprise to most. However, despite this, the role of the Home Guard principally remained the same.

Because the newly named Home Guard still lacked sufficient numbers of weapons, its high-spirited members often had to improvise. While on patrol they would take with them items such as pikes, truncheons, pick-axes, broom handles and even golf clubs! It was reported that in at least one Home Guard unit, the guards took with them on patrol duty packets of pepper which would, if required, be thrown into the eyes of invaders and thus interfere with their vision.

The Home Guard quite rightly occupy a noble place in the history of Britain. Although a certain humour has been associated with it, we would be wise to remember the circumstances under which these brave men volunteered: the enemy was not a myth, but a living, breathing, killing foe, a cruel people who would stop at nothing to achieve the goals set by their evil leaders – and all that parted them from these shores was the Channel. Had Britain been invaded, as seemed more than likely at the time, the Home Guard would have been first to fight and first to die. They deserve our respect and our thanks – we should be proud of such men.

HOME GUARD DUTIES

Being a Home Guard volunteer was far from easy, all but a few members would work all day in their full-time jobs and then (later that evening) take up their Home Guard duties. It was also extremely dangerous too, with some 1206 members killed whilst serving on duty and 557 seriously wounded.

The main duties were:

- Manning of aircraft batteries – Around 142,000 brave men served in this type of post with over 1000 killed whilst on duty.

- Patrolling of waterways (such as canals and rivers), railway stations, coastlines, factories, aerodromes.

- Clearing up debris following air raid attacks.

- Searching through rubble for trapped civilians following air raid attacks.

- Offering (if required) fighting assistance to the army – There was even a Home Guard section of 'Skating Boys' who could deliver this help speedily by 'roller-skating' their way to the place they were called!

- Construction of concrete pill boxes.

- Erecting defence lines including the laying of anti-tank obstacles, barbed wire barriers along beaches and farming implements acting as roadblock checkpoints.

- Placement of obstacles in fields to prevent enemy aircraft from landing.

- Practising of guerrilla tactics/formations – The Home Guard created special secret auxiliary units so that if invasion did happen, they would (in the words of Churchill) 'fight every street of London and suburbs and devour an invading army'.

- Removal of, or blacking out of, signposts.

- Improvement of weapons skills by hours of target practice – Believe it or not, but a German bomber was actually shot down by the rifle fire of the Home Guard after it was sighted flying over a London district!

- Guarding of Buckingham Palace – The Royal Family had its own Home Guard Company which formed part of the 1st County of London (Westminster) Battalion. This particular honour befell the Home Guard in its third year. (King George VI later became Colonel in Chief of the Home Guard.)

- Bomb disposal.

Of course, while recruits enthusiastically carried out their duties, they would always be listening out for the ring of church bells – the pre-arranged signal announcing the start of Germany's invasion.

All of these responsibilities helped to release the regular army to do other equally important tasks. It also helped to boost the morale of troops serving overseas, for they knew a very able force back home was looking after their families.

Despite Hitler and the other fascist armies often sneering at the Home Guard, Hitler (in particular) was all too aware of the growing strength of British Civil Defence.

HOME GUARD 'CALL-UP'

Under the National Service (Number 2) Act of December 1941, male civilians found that they could be ordered to join the Home Guard and attend up to 48 hours training a month. This 'call-up' was quite a surprise especially considering that the numbers of volunteers never fell below one million!

THE HOME GUARD GREW IN STRENGTH

To mark the first anniversary of the Home Guard, a parade was held at Buckingham Palace on the 20th May 1941. With its volunteers totalling 1.5 million at this point in time, the Home Guard was clearly going from strength to strength. In one of Churchill's many speeches, he said of the Home Guard:

'1940. If the enemy had descended suddenly in large numbers from the sky in different parts of the country, they would have found only little clusters of men mostly armed with shotguns, gathered around our search light positions. But now, whenever he comes, if he comes, he will find wherever he should place his foot, that he will be immediately attacked by resolute, determined men who have a perfectly clear intention and resolve to namely put him to death!'

This growing of strength was how it was over the next three years until in late 1944 when they were finally disbanded. With the Battle of Britain long won and invasion looking less and less likely, everybody was now preparing for victory and not invasion. And after 'Operation Overlord', a real feeling of this victory being within Britain's grasp was shared. Even when Hitler unleashed onto the country his V1 and V2 'Terror' weapons resulting in thousands of civilian deaths, Britain's earlier belief in a German invasion was now seen as unrealistic. So on the 3rd December 1944, with a stand down parade of 7,000 men in London, the Home Guard finally bowed out.

The country had always been both proud and grateful for its 'Dad's Army'. King George VI expressed the nations thoughts when he said: 'You have earned in full measure your country's gratitude'.

* It's worth noting that this age band was not always strictly adhered to. The oldest member of the Home Guard (as the LDV was to later become known) was apparently well into his eighties!

VENGEANCE WEAPONS

After the Blitz of 1940, Londoners experienced a kind of rest. Attacks still happened but they were less frequent. Sirens still wailed but they seemed less threatening and many evacuees drifted back to the city. Then, in January 1944, Londoners began to witness a return of the heavy bombing style familiar from the days and nights of the Blitz. The 'Little Blitz', as it was called, lasted from 21st January to 8th April 1944. It was not as bad as the 1940 Blitz but it was bad enough. In the seven raids in February for example, 1000 were killed and 3000 homes in Battersea destroyed.

V1 FLYING BOMBS

Something worse, something more sinister was yet to come – the V1 flying bomb and the V2 rocket (the V standing for Vergeltungswaffe or 'Reprisal Weapon'). The V1 was a pilotless plane that carried on board a cargo of high explosives. The plane was launched and could fly without a pilot until its engine ran out of fuel. Then the V1 would come crashing down to earth, destroying all that lay beneath it.

On the night of 12th June 1944, London experienced its first night of the flying bombs. Then on the 16th a procession of flying bombs came over by day and by night, and for two weeks the attack continued at the rate of about 100 V1 flying bombs a day.

Of the 100 V1s that were directed at London, British fighter planes would bring down on average 30 of these a day. Defences on the ground, Anti-Aircraft guns, would bring down around ten. The other 60 would still get through. Some fell far from London, but around half reached their Greater London target.

In the skies of Croydon, a borough that lay on the V1 route to London, you might be unlucky enough to see nine V1's in the sky at the same time. During 1944, 142 V1s landed on Croydon over a period of 80 days, destroying at least a thousand houses.

A NEW ROLE FOR WOMEN

Before the Second World War, some people believed that a woman's place was in the home. Many firms were reluctant to employ married women. For example, until the Married Women Teachers Sex Disqualification (Removal) Act of 1919, women had to leave teaching when they got married. After 1919, even though it was illegal, some local authorities still placed obstacles in the path of female employees.

The Second World War changed all that. It was a total war that meant everybody was involved. With many men away in the army, navy and air force, women had to take over the jobs they left behind. Women worked everywhere: in the armed forces as drivers, clerks or military police; on the anti-aircraft guns and in ARP control centres; as sand-bag fillers and fire-fighters; in the Women's Voluntary Service (the WVS); in factories, underground and over-ground, producing munitions for the war; on farms in the Land Army growing food for a hungry nation.

Under the National Service Act of 1941, all women between the ages of 18 and 60 had to sign up for some form of work. These figures show how essential the contribution of women was to the whole war effort.

- **December 1942** 8.5 million women, aged 19 to 46, had registered

- **May 1943** 6,311,000 were working in industry or the armed services

- **December 1943** 1.5 million women workers in the engineering industry, 30% of the total workforce

One out of every three workers in the factories was a woman, making the planes, tanks, guns and bullets needed in the war, labouring on heavy industrial machinery that prejudiced people before the war had said was not 'women's work'. To help all the workers in industry, Ernest Bevin (the Minister of Labour) introduced improved welfare facilities in or near the factories. These included proper canteens, nursery schools and medical help.

Women from all social backgrounds became involved. The Ministry of Information followed one upper-class young woman in her duties at a WVS canteen:

'Miss Patience Brand, in the thick of London's society whirl before the war, is now a hard-working Women's Voluntary Services (WVS) worker whose happy smile and unbounding energy have cheered and comforted thousands of blitzed Londoners. Boo Brand is only 18, her friend Rachel Bingham 20. They sleep at the WVS canteen service depot with the alarm set for 2.30am for it is at that unearthly hour that they must get up and get their canteen ready for serving shelterers who leave for work at the crack of dawn. Despite the hour, they get up cheerfully and dress between the pillars reinforcing their sleeping quarters.'

The massive contribution made by women to the war effort was recognised by all. The US War Department offered this advice to American soldiers when they came to Britain in 1942 (quoted in Susan Briggs 'Keep Smiling Through', Fontana 1975):

'British women have proved themselves in this war. They have stuck to their posts near burning ammunition dumps, delivered messages afoot after their motor-cycles have been blasted from under them. There isn't a single record of any British woman in uniformed service quitting her post, or failing in her duty under fire. When you see a girl in uniform with a bit of ribbon on her tunic, remember she didn't get it for knitting more socks than anyone else in Ipswich.'

Gillian Tanner was one of these 'girls in uniform with a bit of ribbon on her tunic', awarded the George Medal as a fire-fighter in the Auxiliary Fire Service. The George Medal is given to civilians only for acts of great courage and bravery where a person has put her or his own life at great risk in order to save others.

WOMEN'S LAND ARMY (WLA) – 'THE FORGOTTEN ARMY…'

The Women's Land Army came from all walks of life and really got stuck in to work for which most of them were, on the face of it, ill equipped. But they soon learned and their contribution to ultimate victory must never be forgotten. Here is a most succinct history of the Land Army for which I thank Wayne and Darren Wilkins of the Home Sweet Home Front website.

LIFE AS A LAND GIRL

The Women's Land Army was made up of girls from every walk of life. Posters of smiling girls bathing in glorious sunshine and open fields covered the fact that the raw recruits (many from industrial towns) were presented with gruelling hard work and monotony.

Homesickness was common as many of the girls had never been away from their parents for long periods. This was particularly true of the girls that stayed in private billets. The girls that stayed in local hostels often told a different story and were more settled as they were grouped together. However, despite all this, there was a great sense of camaraderie amongst the girls who ultimately made life long friends.

ORIGINS

The Women's Land Army, often referred to as 'The Forgotten Army', was actually formed in 1917 by Roland Prothero, the then Minister for Agriculture. The Great War had seen food supplies dwindle and saw the creation of the Women's Land Army (WLA). The WLA was reformed in June 1939 first asking for volunteers and later by conscription with numbers totalling 80,000 by 1944.

WOMEN'S LAND ARMY SONG

Back to the land, we must all lend a hand.
To the farms and the fields we must go.
There's a job to be done,
Though we can't fire a gun
We can still do our bit with the hoe…
Back to the land, with its clay and its sand,
Its granite and gravel and grit,
You grow barley and wheat
And potatoes to eat
To make sure that the nation keeps fit…
We will tell you once more
You can help win the war
If you come with us – back to the land.

Girls had to adjust to Land Army life very quickly and erratic love lives, resentments and bad behaviour all had to be contained. To this end representatives for each county had to be elected. Each county had its organising secretary and local representative. The representative had to ensure that all the girls within their area were content but disciplined. The representative in turn reported to the organising secretary directly, who saw that all conditions of employment were being met. It is important to remember that the WLA was not a military organisation in any way, which was often forgotten by the government.

UNIFORMS

Some girls were attracted to the uniform, others described it as awful! Many agreed that the aertex shirts were scratchy and wearing a tie never seemed to work. The uniforms were normally far too big and breeches had to be taken in, however, resourceful girls normally did their own tailoring and made a good job of improving them. The uniforms normally consisted of:

- 2 short sleeved shirts
- 1 green pullover
- 2 pairs of socks
- 1 pair of shoes
- 1 bib and brace overall
- 1 hat
- 1 pair of rubber boots
- 1 long (very thin!) Mackintosh for the winter

EVENINGS OUT

After working long hours the land girls often looked forward to the free time they were given. Entertainment often came in the form of dances or picture shows in the local village hall. Evenings were also spent writing letters home or reading novels. The local village halls were not always 'local' and girls sometimes had to walk two or three miles to get there. Transport was not always on offer and it meant a long walk home for most. It was only the girls that stayed in the hostels that might be lucky in guaranteeing some kind of transport home. However, to others just a hot bath seemed like heaven after a tiring day toiling!

CHRISTMAS ON THE HOME FRONT

Human nature is strange, people are strange. We place labels on arbitrary units of time which are in themselves meaningless: days, hours, minutes and seconds. They are the heartbeat of our lives. In war these can seem longer or shorter depending on circumstances. A 48 hour pass seemed to some service men and women to last a second, yet the same period of time in a cold barracks crawled along like a lifetime. In the broader picture Christmas was a significant marker to use. The desire was for the whole damn thing to be 'over by Christmas'. However unlikely an end to the conflict seemed there was always the glimmer of hope that families would be together safe and warm around a lit tree and a steaming turkey and pudding.

There were to be six Wartime Christmases; six aiming points to peace – none of which were accurate. It goes some way to demonstrating what it was about the British people that enabled them to see it through that they, when they could, kept Christmas well, or as well as could be expected.

BOMBS, RATIONING, THE BLACKOUT AND CHRISTMAS CHEER!

Although the war on the Home Front brought with it unimaginable hardships particularly as the war dragged on, Christmas was a time where people tried to forget these hardships and remember what it was like before the bombs, rationing and blackouts.

Even though food was short many people still managed to find a turkey, chicken, duck, goose or pheasant for their Christmas lunch which helped to supplement the endless mountains of carrots and potatoes. As was highlighted with the Dr Carrot advertising campaign the former were supposed to help improve people's night vision and prevent unnecessary accidents in the blackout. It is a sad fact that many people were killed during the early days of the blackout as a result of walking in front of moving cars.

In the absence of fresh tropical fruits, carrots were also used to help flavour cakes. Mince pies were always a traditional Christmas treat so housewives made do and improvised. It was suggested that mincemeat could go that little bit further if grated or finely diced apple or apple pulp was added to the ingredients. If mincemeat was not available then spices could be added with dried fruit, dates or cooked prunes.

CHRISTMAS TREES AND DECORATIONS

It was impossible to get a tree for Christmas because of the timber restrictions, and even those who were fortunate to find one paid extortionate prices. They were often disappointed because these trees were merely smaller cut offs of bigger trees.

If you were lucky enough to have a Christmas tree then the authorities sternly reminded you that it was inadvisable to use candles on the trees as you never knew when a German bomb might cause an electrical blackout and these candles might be needed.

As for Christmas decorations these were seen as luxury items and not available in the shops. Most people just relied on their old decorations that they had purchased before the war. These were enough to help spread a little bit of Christmas cheer.

Christmas was a particularly difficult time for children, especially those that had been evacuated and were now living in strange homes far away from their parents.

For those that were still with their parents, toys were scarce with all the toyshops displaying empty shelves. After all kapok was needed more for lifejackets than for teddy bears!

GAMES AT CHRISTMAS

For some, indulgence was simply a quiet time at home with loved ones and the radio. For others, card games such as Rummy were the order of the day, or reading out loud to each other. All in all the British people made do and celebrated Christmas as best they could, praying that the hostilities in Europe and all over the world would soon be at an end.

Part Two

THEY WERE THERE

'Potato Pete'

Part Two
THEY WERE THERE

A collection of accounts by people who experienced the effects
of the war first hand.

A MOTHER'S STORY

'At the end of August 1939, we were told to pack suitcases for the
children and prepare for their evacuation from London. I had five
children. Joan (13) and John (11) the two oldest reported to their
schools for the trip into the unknown. I took the younger ones, Eileen
(9), Leslie (7) and Margaret (5), to their school. They had name tickets
pinned to their coats and carried their boxed gas masks on a string
around their necks. There was a long line of buses ready to take them
away and the police on duty, told us to turn our backs, so as not to
upset the children if we could not hold back the tears. We had no
idea where they were to be taken and it was a most dreadful feeling,
losing my five children in one day.

POSTERS DESIGNED TO MOTIVATE THE WORKFORCE

A few days later we were told the whereabouts of our children. Joan in Brighton, John in Burwash, Sussex, Eileen, Leslie and Margaret had been taken to Hailsham, Sussex. With the children gone, I felt completely at a loss. Eventually the schools arranged coach trips on Sunday's and we were able to visit the children in their 'foster homes'.

Joan seemed happy in Brighton, but John would turn away from us so that we could not see his tears. He was very unhappy in his first billet and finally told his father about the bullying from two older lads in the family he was lodged with. My husband arranged for him to be moved and he found a warm welcome at his next 'home'. The three youngest were also very unhappy, billeted with a child-less couple who did not show them any affection.

The children were made to move again when the Battle of Britain started. Many children ignoring the Government warnings, had returned to London and we were very glad that the children were safe in South Wales when the bombing started in earnest.

Young John was sent to Garnant, a mining village near Ammanford, where he seemed reasonably happy, Eileen went to Abergwili, a small town about four miles from Carmarthan, where she was billeted with a wonderful family, Mr and Mrs Dawkins. Leslie was taken to live on a farm in the Welsh hills and Margaret to an isolated house next to the church in a place called Nanty-Couse, where she learned to speak Welsh.

When Eileen found where Margaret was living, Mrs Dawkins decided to make a visit. She later gave me a very funny account of that day. The address was 'The Manse' so she made sure that they were dressed suitably to visit what she thought was a vicarage. Imagine her astonishment when they arrived to find everything in the place covered with feathers as the woman was plucking chickens.

The house was a complete mess, Margaret was running around in the yard outside in dirty old clothes, playing with her foster brothers. This was no vicarage, so all Mrs Dawkins' efforts to impress were wasted.

SALVAGE 1940'S STYLE

I was still living in London with John, my husband, the bombing had increased and I was now six months pregnant. John had received orders to report to Greenock in Scotland as the London Docks where he worked as a stevedore were under constant attack. So I went to stay with Margaret in Nanty-Couse and although I hated it, at least my new baby would be safe. Helen, my new daughter was born in Carmarthan Hospital on December 7th 1940, but when I returned to the lodgings in Nanty-Couse, I found that the landlady's children had chicken pox.

Once again, Mrs Dawkins came to the rescue, offering me a place to live in Abergwili, until I could find somewhere of my own. I managed to rent two rooms with a Mrs Plummer and with Eileen just a few hundred yards away, we were more like a family again. Helen was an attractive baby and Mrs Dawkins, who acted as godparent, bought many clothes for her, they called her 'Dimples' and wanted to adopt her.

Margaret, at my insistence, had been moved and was living on a farm owned by the brother of Leslie's foster parents. She seemed very happy there, riding a horse to school each day. However a very mature 14 year old 'Liverpudlian ' evacuee came to lodge there. I noticed some very bad bruises on Margaret's back when she was trying on some undergarments that I had made for her. I discovered that every Saturday night, when the foster parents were out, this girl made Margaret sit in a bath of very hot water, then put in her bed, made to sit up in the bed and go to sleep. Everytime she moved or threatened to tell of her treatment, she was beaten with a towel holder that the older girl had secreted in her chest of drawers. My complaint, to the school, led to the evacuee confessing and she was expelled from the school.

I earned a little money by cleaning the flat of two school teachers, Miss Tinley and Mrs Cato. My husband John would visit as often as he could and he became great friends with Mr Dawkins. We kept in touch with the wonderful Dawkins family for many years.

Joan, my eldest daughter, came to live with me, until she left school and joined the WAAFS when she reached the age of 18. In September 1941, Eileen was moved to Llanelly. She had won a scholarship to Mary Datchelor School.

In February 1941, I found that I was pregnant again. I returned to the flat in Peckham, South London, taking Helen with me. Son John who was now 14, returned with me, as the bombing had finished, apart from a few sneak attacks – or so we thought.

August 1942, and Eileen was allowed to come home to help me through the pregnancy and on September 16th 1942, son David was born. I was now 43 years of age. Eileen returned to her school in Llanelly, John my eldest son, stayed in London to help me look after the two babies, Helen and David. In September 1943, Margaret joined Eileen at Mary Datchelor School. They both stayed with a Mrs Jones, another fine lady who was kind to the Roberts family.

In February 1944, our flat in Peckham suffered a direct hit and was destroyed and members of the family injured. My husband who was still working in Scotland urged me to return to Wales, so on a day in June I went back to the kind people of South Wales, taking Helen and David with me. John stayed in London assuring me that he could look after himself.

That day as I discovered when I got back to Wales was D-Day, the 6th June 1944.'

MRS LILIAN ROBERTS

UNWELCOME GUESTS DROP IN   LOCATION CHANNEL ISLANDS

The first German invaders were dropped by parachute onto Guernsey on June 30th 1940. Copies of an ultimatum which were also dropped gave instructions that white crosses were to be painted on prominent parts of the island and white flags flown from public buildings to show unconditional surrender. Thus began a painful time for the occupants of the Islands.

Here are the memories of a witness to these events:

'It was a funny time for my family. We had no idea that we would be invaded. My dad's pal was a navy man and had written to us a few weeks before the Germans came. He said as how it was impossible that Jerry would be allowed to attack Jersey. My dad was always saying how Britain would send out some gunboats to see off Jerry if he came. That was not how it all turned out. We were all wrong.'

JAGO

EDGAR'S STORY   LOCATION CHANNEL ISLANDS

It has been difficult to find people from the Channel Islands who are prepared to talk frankly about life during the Occupation. It is apparent that there are many dark secrets to be kept. Here 'Edgar' tells his story:

'I remember the day very well. I had been out with my cousin John. Just hanging about looking around. We had not seen so many foreigners before the Germans arrived. All the kids I knew had been told to watch what we did and to stay out of the Germans' way as much as we could. Then, after a few weeks, I came home from school and there was a German sergeant sitting at our table. My aunt Janet had brought him round for tea. He was a huge man with short hair and smelled of sweat and gun oil. I went into the kitchen to see my mother and she was not happy. She told me to go upstairs and stay

THE INVASION OF THE CHANNEL ISLANDS

there until the German had gone. He stayed until about eight o'clock and my mother and father had words about it all. My mother said what could she do as her sister had started to go with the soldier and said that we would just have to put up with it as the Germans were in charge now. That was the start of some very bad days for my family as my aunt had many friends who went with Germans and she brought many to our house. They treated my home as if they owned it. One of my aunt's German's friends used to stay over in our spare room with his girlfriend without even asking permission. Sometimes they were very nasty to us and rude. Although there were stories that they had been told not to be nasty to the Islanders some were. One of them told stories about how he had worked with some of the forced labour and how he liked to beat them. He said he hated the Jews and loved it when he could really beat them badly. My aunt used to sit on his lap and agree with everything he said. It made my parents very angry. There were so many girls going out with Germans and so many children as a result. When the Germans first invaded my parents had told us that we would do all we could to keep out of their way and hope that the Islands would be liberated soon. A lot of Islanders we knew thought the same but a lot didn't. And when the Germans came they took them into their homes and beds without much hesitation. It made us all ashamed to be Islanders. After the war we left Jersey for the mainland. My parents found it hard to be nice to some of the collaborators and thought it better to make a clean start. My dad didn't even like taking their money for the work he did for them.

Many years later we went back for a family holiday. It was no surprise to find that people did not like us to talk about the occupation. It seems as if as there are so many Islanders now with German blood in them that do not know it, it is hoped that if no one talks about it very often less of the truth would come out. It was a horrible time, the Occupation, that showed a very ugly side to some of the Islanders, particularly the women.'

EDGAR

RUNNING A PIGGERY   LOCATION LONDON

'My brother was in the Civil Defence. A lot of the time he spent helping to run the group piggery which they had been allowed to build on a very small part of Tooting Bec Common. The pigs were fed mainly on kitchen scraps, which the members of the group had to collect, upon which the animals appeared to thrive. All of the pigs went into the official swim but some pork was returned and shared out amongst members which was welcome at times like Christmas'.

GEORGE KNOTT

BATTLE OF BRITAIN   LOCATION LONDON

'Right after Neville Chamberlain's declaration of war on Germany the air-raid sirens sounded. Everyone rushed out into the street at the sound of aircraft, but it turned out to be just a couple of Spitfires flying fairly low overhead. The first job was to hang up damp blankets over the windows and doors, which was supposed to protect us from a gas attack – whether it would have worked or not no-one knew! Then of course every window had to be blacked out with dark curtains so that no light would show to the outside, and ARP wardens and police patrolled the streets shouting 'Put that light out' wherever they saw a chink of light. I even did this later in the war as an Air Cadet. Many windows were criss-crossed with masking tape to prevent glass flying in the event of a nearby bomb burst.

My first memories of the Battle of Britain in 1940 was of seeing contrails high in the sky where Spitfires and Hurricanes were attacking the German bombers. Some of them came down quite low from time to time and we often saw a He 111 being shot at by fighters on its tail and at least one German bomber being shot down in Pym's park. Another vivid memory is of a lone Stuka flying down the High Street, Wood Green, at almost rooftop height, machine gunning everything as it flew by. We could see the crew's faces, which was a common sight for friendly aircraft but a rarity for enemy aircraft! Some of the enemy aircraft had sirens and many had loudspeakers attached to their engines in order to create more terror among the populace below.

Some of our parks, Broomfield Park for instance, had tree trunks sticking up into the air at a 45° angle loosely camouflaged with nets – apparently to make the enemy bomber crews think that these were anti-aircraft guns.

Many people went down into the Underground railway for shelter, but we did not. At first, as soon as the sirens sounded we sheltered from the bombing in a sort of corrugated iron Anderson shelter covered with earth at the bottom of the garden, and more than once said 'goodbye' to each other when the action was heavy and the bombs falling close by. However, it had a stale smell inside, it was necessary to empty the water from the sump frequently and all in all it was a miserable experience, especially at night with the dog curled up inside too, howling at the bomb blasts and anti-aircraft guns replete with flashes of 'lightning.' Therefore after about a week of this we went back into the house and slept under a marble billiard table until that too soon became quite a chore and we finally went back upstairs to bed. It was sometimes hard to sleep in the noise and flashes of the guns, and especially so when a Bofors gun was put on rails and manned at the open Underground line near Arnos Grove tube station. After heavy ack-ack fire there was always a smell of cordite in the air. We often saw German aircraft caught in the searchlights. As soon as one searchlight found a 'plane, all the others would converge on it and the aircraft started weaving and dodging all over the sky but travelled far away or was shot down before the searchlights lost it.

School was as often cancelled as not, and many of the regular teachers were in the armed forces, so we basically had elderly ladies or disabled veterans from WW I for teachers. Most of my contemporaries hated school, with its penchant for corporal punishment, and many times I can remember riding my bike to almost within shouting distance of the main gate when the air-raid siren would go off and I would turn around and cycle back home through the raid rather than go inside the school. Caning was prevalent, one on each hand for asking what the teacher considered a stupid question, the same punishment for talking in class or 'answering back' (trying to be smart with the teacher) as it was called, six strokes on the behind for being late for class, two to four strokes for not completing our homework and sometimes an ear or two boxed if we didn't pay attention. Thus school became a painful experience in more ways than one. Our 'playtime' consisted mainly of playing tag in the playground, sometimes kicking a football around; playing marbles in the street and sometimes in class (!); using rubber bands to catapult wet paper darts at each other during boring class periods; using small round oil cans with a long spout as water pistols; building working but useless models out of paper clips; cycling everywhere within a 30 mile radius; fishing with a line on a wood bracket and a bent pin; roller skating in the street; 'scrumping' apples, pears and walnuts and being chased off the property by the local policeman; the weekly football or cricket game and a once-in-a-while excursion to the local swimming baths, more frequently in the summer. I attended four schools between 1939 and 1946, and I can honestly say that they were all alike in this regard, only the buildings and very few of the teachers were different. We almost cheered when teachers began to return from the forces in 1945-6. School became a totally different experience and for the first time in years we felt that we were beginning to learn something.

Boys wore short pants and long socks in winter and summer, and a boy's 13th birthday with the traditional present of his first pair of long trousers was something to celebrate! At grammar school we were required to wear a cap and blue blazer with the school badge embroidered on them. In poor weather we were able to ride the bus to school for one penny rather than cycle. We also used to frequent a stationers/tobacconists where, after we had bought our first comic book for two pence, we were able to 'trade it in' on another one for a penny and buy a packet of sherbet for another halfpenny. As I approached 17 and graduation, we were taken on excursions to various factories, coal mines, company offices and so forth ostensibly to find out what interested us for a career. The numbers of aircraft I had seen over the past several years undoubtedly influenced my decision to fly for the RAF, which I did.

Most of the boys built solid model aircraft, a few built flying models with a .049 engine whose propeller could snap back and really hurt your fingers if you weren't careful starting it. We collected and traded shrapnel and pieces of shell casing, nose cones, clips of machine-gun bullets, small aircraft parts sometimes with German printing on it, and incendiary bomb fins found on the streets and in the parks. I was a volunteer 'victim' at a local hospital for trainee nurses to bandage up, and during one raid, as I was on my way to the first aid station, I 'collected' a piece of red hot shrapnel from the ack-ack guns in my knee and ended up being treated for real by the same nurses who had practiced on me earlier, including an aunt who had 'volunteered' me for this task. After school we sometimes watched the REME personnel defusing unexploded bombs from a cordoned-off barrier plainly marked UXB, and went to see bomb damaged houses and fires still burning. One cul-de-sac near our house was completely demolished by an aerial land mine dropped by parachute, strips of the 'chute still visible in the trees.

Although we could easily see the London Dockland burning from our bedroom window, the worst that happened to my family was a piece of the Underground railway concrete coming through a bedroom window when a bomb landed on the platform after traversing the air shaft. Many people sheltering in the deep tunnel were killed and ambulances with first aid people picking up bodies and body parts were kept busy for days. However, my future wife's flat was set on fire by incendiaries while she was sheltering in the basement with her parents, and the thing that she most vividly remembers about that incident was being unable to climb the stairs to save any personal possessions since the stairwell was on fire and all the firemen were busy putting out fires elsewhere! Her family lost everything except the clothes on their backs, they had to spend two nights in a 'refugee' shelter and then find accommodation out of town since nothing was available in the city.

One of the most frightening experiences that I remember was seeing a huge flaming ball slowly fall from the sky. I had no idea what it was, it was as if the sun was falling. As I stood in awe watching it descend, another bystander told me that it was a barrage balloon which had been shot down and the gas was burning. The local park had a barrage balloon unit and often we would watch the personnel send this up and lower it, and this was apparently shot down by enemy aircraft although we didn't see it happen.

Another frightening experience was when the local bottle factory was hit by bombs and glass flew in every direction for hundreds of yards. Some diamond-shaped pieces of glass about a foot square stuck into the sides of trees, so strong was the blast. If anyone had been standing there it would probably have cut their head off.

V2 ON ITS MOBILE LAUNCH VEHICLE

While the Blitz was bad enough, worse was yet to come. We began to see flying bombs, the infamous V1 or Vergeltungswaffe Eins (Revenge Weapon 1) which often flew over the rooftops well under 1000 feet. As long as the engine was running, with a sort of sput-sput-sput sound, the bomb would continue its flight and there was no danger. As soon as the engine stopped, the bomb would fall, usually severely damaging two or three houses. Some did actually hit a military target, such as one that fell on Standard Telephone and Cables Company, but for the most part they were merely terror weapons. Many were shot down by anti-aircraft guns and fighter aircraft, some Gloster Meteors being able to catch up to them and tip their wings over so that they crashed in the fields. Later came the V2, which was a 3000 mph rocket and against which there was no defence. They also mostly hit houses, but one hit a synagogue close by our house and dozens of cans of meat which had been stored in the basement were strewn all over the street which people almost fought over to retrieve, any kind of meat being very scarce. We did get canned powdered (dehydrated) egg from the USA as well as canned mashed potatoes called POM, but the taste was nothing like the real thing. Also the US Army used to make doughnuts at Lyons Corner House in Leicester Square and freely distributed them to the British public. American soldiers and airmen were everywhere and easy to strike up a conversation with. They always had plenty of chocolate and chewing gum for the children and cigarettes for the adults. Many were invited into our homes for tea and biscuits and usually proved to be very generous and interesting people to talk to.

Rationing of food and practically everything else was a big problem for everyone. Those who could afford it purchased food on the Black Market. My parents paid 12 shillings for a dozen eggs which normally sold for one shilling in the shops – if you could get them. Clothing and petrol were rationed and everyone had little ration books with perforated coupons which had to be given up as one purchased items, and this continued into the 1950's. [I have a picture of one of these]. Long lines for seemingly everything were the norm, and I can remember lining up for over half an hour to buy some cigarettes for my father only to be told that they were sold out before I got to the counter. Since almost everyone smoked in those days, especially men, cigarettes and tobacco were in great demand. One time the USAAF dropped flour bombs in a field for bombing practice, and a number of us teenagers collected up as much as we could and took it home, as pure white flour was never seen in the shops. In 1944 my uncle brought home some white loaves of bread from his ship and we couldn't believe the whiteness of it, we hadn't seen anything like that in years. He also brought back nylon stockings from New York and the ladies went wild over them. I had seen girls fighting over parachute silk taken from aerial land mines, so ready made nylons were a prized item.

USAAF CREW LEATHERCLAD FOR BATTLE

I was an avid cyclist in those days and would often go 30 or 40 miles on a weekend to Southend and to various airfields around the greater London area. There we watched the fighters take off and land and later the bombers, especially the USAAF B-17 Fortresses which often returned badly damaged. Security was not considered a problem in those days and we were allowed to wander around almost at will, often getting chocolate and chewing gum from the American airmen. My uncle played baseball for the Hornsey Red Sox during his leaves from the Navy and many times played against the Americans. I acted as a 'ball boy' recovering balls that were hit outside the boundary and would receive as much as two shillings from the Americans for retrieving a single ball. When you consider that I was paid a total of only seven shillings a week for both morning and evening newspaper rounds, this was a great deal of money to me, and I could often make more on a weekend than I made all week with my 'paper rounds.

Everyone was required to carry gas masks everywhere they went, and the police would sometimes set off a tear gas canister in a busy shopping area to make sure that everyone did indeed carry one with them! There was also a 'gasmask' unit which my baby brother was put in, looking something like an alien from outer space – a Perspex window was provided so that my parents could see him. If he had needed feeding or changing during a gas attack, I don't know what would have happened. Fortunately we never experienced poison gas attacks as my Father had in the First World War.

We read about the war in the newspapers and listened to the BBC, also to Lord Haw Haw (William Joyce) who tried to convince us that it was useless to continue the fight. Sometimes we would listen to Hitler's speeches and although nobody spoke a word of German they would try to pick out place names and words which sounded similar to English. Whether they meant the same was anybody's guess. Our radios were often powered by what we called 'accumulators' and every week these were exchanged for a fully charged one at the local hardware store.

In 1940 the Alexandra Palace became a staging area for troops returning from Dunkirk, and since the Palace was a favourite haunt of adults and children alike, we watched these soldiers returning, many with bandaged heads and bodies, but all seemingly quite cheerful and probably feeling lucky that they were alive. They passed out cigarettes to everyone, even gave out clips of rifle ammunition to the kids as souvenirs, something that I'm sure wouldn't be tolerated today.

Whenever we went to the coast for a day or two, it was impossible to get on the beaches as they were cordoned off by barbed wire, anti-tank traps, light howitzers and soldiers patrolling the front. There were even anti-tank traps in London at the side of the roads with concrete 'pegs' set in the ground which could be easily removed and the triangular iron traps set up. The worst part about the coast was the frequent 'tip and run' raiders who would fly across the Channel at low level, climb up to drop a couple of 500lb bombs and then dart back down and back across the sea before anyone realised what was happening. Sometimes we saw already-airborne Spitfires chase them, but never saw one shot down.'

BEWARE

HE WANTS TO KNOW YOUR UNIT'S NAME.
WHERE YOU'RE GOING, WHENCE YOU CAME.
EVEN ALONE OR IN A CROWD
NEVER MENTION THESE OUT LOUD.

SOME WALLS HAVE EARS

OTHER MEMORIES   LOCATION LONDON

Victory gardens on tiny allotments by the railroad lines, where people grew vegetables.

Posters everywhere exhorting us to 'Eat more Bread,' and warning posters such as 'Loose Lips Sink Ships' with caricatures of Hitler lying under a restaurant table listening to the conversation of the diners.

Memories of furniture stores building the wooden Mosquito parts, and bombed out shops with often humourous signs stating that they were still in business and ready to serve the public.

I remember collecting farthings and had almost £10 worth at the end of the war (about 9,600 of them!) probably worth £100 in today's money.

Scouts with six foot long staves which we used for everything from climbing and measuring distances to just pole-vaulting around on the way to and from Scout meetings.

ATC (Air Training Corps) with a first flight in an Avro Anson in 1944 in which the pilot let me 'take the controls,' and Air Raid Precaution duties complete with stirrup pump and tin helmet which was heavy and uncomfortable. Also aircraft recognition classes which enabled those who passed the exams to be nominated 'Spotters' who called out enemy or friendly aircraft to the school population via a Tannoy broadcasting system.

Others include watching iron railings, pots and pans being collected to help with metal shortages for the war effort, and exhibitions of German aircraft which had been shot down. A sixpenny entrance fee was usually charged which supposedly went to some good cause to help the war effort.

The 'Home Guard' which was first called the Local Defence Volunteers with an LDV armband, civilian suits and broomsticks for rifles as they paraded in the school playgrounds. My father, a World War I veteran was a member of this group and learned unarmed combat at 42 years of age! I believe he was finally issued a uniform in 1942 and a WWI Lee Enfield rifle in 1944, long after any threat of invasion had passed! No one ever seemed to know where the ammunition was kept!

Most of all, I remember the good humour and general upbeat spirit of the people, most of whom continued their work in sometimes extreme difficulties under fire, acting as though defeat was unthinkable and who most likely would have gone on fighting even if the Germans had invaded our island.'

JIM WILCOX, NANAIMO, B.C. CANADA.

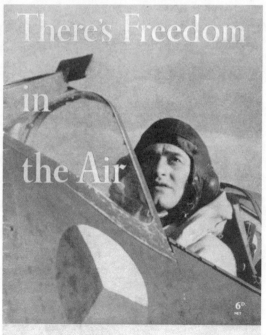

COVER OF 'OFFICIAL STORY OF ALLIED AIR FORCES'.

THE SAGA OF 'MY BUDDY'

The bravery of the men of the USAAF is legendary and the number of stories I could have included is high. I have had to be selective and it has been one of the hardest of all tasks. The story of 'My Buddy' is one that I found most evocative (I have not edited it in any way) therefore I have given over much space to the telling of it. This is the story of a young warrior class who through sheer guts and bravery, that I cannot even begin to understand, fought battles so bloody, so costly, so terrible they in their own way wrote across the skies of the world 'Never again, but if we have to we shall'.

"I am writing this introduction to 'The Saga of My Buddy' because all of her crew are now gone and there is no one to tell this touching story. I'd like to set the stage for a letter, written by Leon Finneran who was the engineer and top turret gunner on 'My Buddy' on the day she went down. His letter was written in 1987, shortly before his death, and was addressed to one of the other surviving crew members, Donald Boyle, flying tail gunner on that mission.

This letter tells in detail the experiences of one man who survived a deadly, harrowing experience while flying in combat. It is a story that all of us who flew in B-17's can relate to."

My Buddy' was a B-17, s/n 42-31552 , of the 748th Squadron and on this fateful date was flown by Lt Gerald Kerr and his crew. The mission was to Munich on July 12th, 1944.

This is Leon Finneran's letter to Don Boyle...

'Hi Don,

Sorry for the delay in answering your letter. My wife and I went on a few days vacation for the holiday weekend. Now that everything is back to normal, I will try to answer some of the questions you probably have been asking yourself all these years about the rest of the crew and the plane. Bear in mind my memory isn't what it was then. I will tell you now what I remember at the time of seeing the burst of AA (Anti-aircraft fire) that got us.

We were on the bomb run and I had the turret facing straight ahead. I saw about three shells break in front of us, each one getting nearer the plane. The last shell (which one, whether the 3rd or 4th, I can't remember) hit us and knocked out both our outboard engines. Lindskoog (Co-pilot) immediately began to try to restart one of the engines. I could see gas was pouring over the starboard wing. I reminded Kerr that trying to restart the engines might start a fire. He then feathered both engines. There was no hope of getting home but Kerr said he thought we could make it to Switzerland. We couldn't hold our altitude so Kerr ordered us to throw out everything we could find to lighten the plane.

After pulling out of formation, Kerr told me to get the flare gun and continue to fire hoping we could find fighter protection. I did this and it seemed almost immediately we had fighters on each wing. Kerr was talking to the pilot on our left wing using the FM radio and asked for an escort to Switzerland. They headed us toward the Swiss border but after some time the pilot told Kerr that with all the cloud cover he could not be sure whether or not we were over Switzerland, but thought we were very near the border. The fighter pilot wished us luck and left us. I was standing between Kerr and Lindskoog looking at the clouds below and wondering how we were going to get down through them safely. I was talking to Kerr about the conditions and how we were still losing altitude when one of the other members of the crew said over the intercom that he saw a hole in the cloud cover and that he could see mountains. I then also saw a break in the clouds and told him that I could see we were below the peaks. He then pushed the light signal to prepare to bail out and almost immediately sounded the bail out signal (the bell). He asked me to stay a little longer to see if we could get down. (At this point the four gunners in the back of the plane bailed out but for some reason no one in the front of the plane did... electing to stay with the pilot.) I believe he knew none of us would have much of a chance if he left the controls.

We were flying blind and still losing altitude. I don't know how long it was but I noticed we were beginning to lose oil pressure on the overworked #3 engine. It acted like it was about to give out. There was no way of knowing what damage the flak had done to the two engines that were still operating.

Not being much of a hero, I told Kerr I didn't think we were going to make it and I thought it was time for me to jump. He agreed. I went forward to the nose hatch, put on my 'chute pack and released the hatch. Lindskoog, who followed me down, was kneeling beside the hatch waiting for me to go. The nose hatch looked too small so I took off one of my flying boots. Lindskoog reminded me I might break my foot without my boots so I left the other one on and went headfirst out the nose. Lindskoog jumped after me, but I don't know if his 'chute didn't open or if he was too low (the search party later found his body on the shore of Lake Constance). I flipped over in the air and pulled the ripcord and the pilot 'chute came out but it seemed to me real slow. I started to panic and pulled at the parachute cloth. The 'chute opened and at the same moment I heard the sound of the plane crashing. It's hard to describe how you feel at a time like that because I knew there was no way the others could have gotten out. I knew that none of them survived. I experienced an odd feeling as I floated down. After I heard the plane hit, it was as if I was in a vacuum, no sound, nothing, it seemed so quiet that if someone whispered miles away I would have heard it.

It seemed like only a few seconds after I pulled the cord that I could see I was headed for the side of a mountain. I tried to control my direction but it didn't do any good. My 'chute caught on the peak and I was knocked very hard against the side of the mountain. I don't know how long I was out but when I came to I found the ripcord was still in my tightly clenched fist. The clouds had almost gone and I could see across the valley and I could see our burning plane. I was high on some Swiss mountain in the middle of July and there was snow all around me. I don't think I have ever felt as alone in my life, not knowing where you guys were, and knowing what had just happened to the others.

My 'chute was caught on the peak and there was no way I could get it down. On one side of the slope was snow, on the other, after I looked, was a sheer drop of about three or four thousand feet. The trouble with the snow side was I had to brace my back against the mountain and go side ways on top of the snow an inch at a time. If I slipped it was a quick ride to somewhere... I didn't want to find out where. After reaching a level spot and removing my parachute harness, I took the top part of my underwear off and wrapped it around the foot with no boot and with a lot of Irish luck slowly made my way down into the valley. I broke into a barn and slept in the loft that night. If anyone had said one word to me at that time I think I would have jumped through the roof of the barn.

The next day I took my escape kit maps and compass out and plotted my course. Before going into the service I was a city boy, I knew nothing about a compass or about reading a map. Nevertheless, there I was in the barn with everything laid out as if I was Columbus about to discover the New World. Needless to say, the course I took was later proved completely wrong. (When I was picked up by the Swiss border guards, I was heading back into Germany).

Sometime before I met any border guards, I walked quite a way thinking I was headed into Switzerland. The next day I came across a small cabin with all the windows boarded up. I had plenty to drink from the stream coming down the mountains. I must have been out of shape on the trip because I fell quite a few times and could only walk a few minutes at a time. My head still hurt from the landing so that could have been the reason. I found a pick near the cabin and broke one of the boarded up side windows. I hadn't eaten in a couple of days so I looked for food. There were canned goods on a shelf but I couldn't read the labels so I was still hungry. There were four big bunks against the wall with straw in them, so I took a big knife from the drawer in a table and stuck it in the straw beside me when I laid down.

I don't know how long I was asleep but the next thing I knew the door opens and three men in uniform come in. They put their rifles in the corner and started to take their coats off. They still hadn't noticed me as the side boards on the bunk were high. When you were captured you said you thought they were Swiss guards, in my case I thought they were German soldiers (Swiss and German uniforms are similar). As I said, not being much of a hero, I let go of the knife and made a little noise but did not move out of the bunk. I told them I was American and when they pointed to the buttons on their uniform (Swiss cross) I almost laughed out loud. They gave me cheese, wine and raw bacon. (My mother would not believe me because I cut all fat off any meat I eat.) When we left, one of the older guards (over 50) gave me his shoes and socks and went barefooted. One gave me his jacket because he said we were only 200 yards from the Germans and if they thought I was American they might shoot.

The next day they sent me to a Swiss hospital to have my head x-rayed and in a couple days I was with other American crews that had landed in Switzerland. I was interned for about 6 months until four of us got in touch with the French resistance fighters who took us through the German lines and we made it back to England. After leaving Switzerland we stayed on the outskirts of Nancy, France near the Swiss border. We were later taken to Lyons and flown from there to England. From England I went home for a few weeks and then to Atlantic City for R&R.

It feels good after all these years to tell my experiences to someone who cares. I know you want to know about the officers too.

A couple days after being placed with the Americans, I was told that the Swiss found our wrecked plane. They were going to bury the three officers the next day . They were Kerr, Levine and Shilling (they could not locate Lindskoog's body since he was not with the plane wreckage). I went to the funeral with officers from the American Embassy and a Swiss honour guard. They played Taps and had the Swiss Army fire a last salvo for them. They found Lindskoog some time later and he was given the same burial service. They were all buried in a small Swiss town called Thun.

To this day I can't get over how lucky I was. By all rights, I should have been with you men, or with the real unlucky ones, the officers. Your luck was bad, mine got better.(Editors note – The four enlisted men who bailed out when the order was given by Kerr, were Boyle, Ahlfors, Younger and Hegedus. They too landed in the mountains but on the German side of the Swiss border and were taken prisoner and ended up in the prison camp at Stalag Luft #4 and endured considerable hardship before they were freed.)

That about does it Don. You made a mistake when you asked me to tell you everything that happened after you jumped. If you tell someone about what happened on that last mission, they listen but unless you've been through it, no one really cares, so I hope it sheds some light on what you wanted to know. In my mind I've gone over that mission hundreds of times and still can't get over how lucky I was. Lucky not jumping and becoming a POW. Lucky not waiting too long and ending up with the others. It was only a matter of seconds that I missed ending up with them. Compared to what you guys went through, my experience wasn't much.

I remember some details as if they were yesterday... Kerr saying 'Okay, you had better go too' and I know that Lindskoog's last words to anyone was when he told me I might break my foot in landing without my boots. I still feel sad seeing him kneeling beside the nose hatch talking to me and waiting for me to jump. I still feel sad that we never shook hands or wished each other luck, I hope it was because we were either scared or being young never thought anything bad could happen to us and would see each other on the ground. It's been a long time to say it, but I'm happy for every one of you that made it out. Maybe not in the best of health, but at least alive. After all these years it feels good to tell of my experiences to someone who cares. Hoping to hear from you soon.

Your friend from another time, Lee Finneran'

LEE FINNERAN

SCHOOL DAYS – 1939 TO 1948 LOCATION KENT/LONDON

'The school that I went to was very different to schools today, unless you managed to get a scholarship, you stayed with the same school until you left, in my case that was age 15.

I was just five years old when I started school. My class had about 40 children, and the first half of the morning session was spent with play learning, I was lucky, my dad had taught me to read and write a little, he also taught me the alphabet and my two times table, so I had a bit of an advantage. After playtime, we learned country dancing and keep fit, we used to call it exercises. I would go home for my dinner, I only lived across the road from the school, the first session in the afternoon was spent with more play learning and then we used to sleep on little camp beds for about an hour. The teacher used to have one of the head girls to help her to keep us in order. Our classroom was a large room with lots of windows, there all sorts of things for us to play with, but one thing has always stayed in my mind, a big rocking horse, you could get three children on it, one on the horse and two on baskets at either end of the horse. Nothing very eventful happened up to September. Then the war started. There was lots of drills about what to do if there was an air-raid. A bell would ring and we all had to line up and walk steadily to the air-raid shelter. This was a cellar under the main school. When I look back on this time, we wouldn't have stood a chance if there had been a direct hit, but we all felt quite safe because we didn't know any better. One rule that always had to be obeyed at all times, you never went anywhere without your gas mask.

There was a fire station just round the corner from our school, we were taken there and had our gas masks tested, we had to go in a special van type vehicle, I have never been too sure how the masks were tested, the room seem to go all smokey and we were told to breath normally. Whatever it was we all survived.

With the start of the war, things changed quite a lot, as children were evacuated, that meant that a lot of the schools were half empty, so some were temporarily closed and the children all put together in other schools. I was evacuated for the first time as the war started so didn't get involved with this change. I was only away for about 6/8 weeks (I wanted to come home), when I came home my school was opened again.

Each year we went up to another class, at the end of each year, the school put up a list of names and how well they had done, I was always third or fourth, couldn't quite manage any more than that. The war changed what we did, we still had our lessons, but a lot of time was spent trying to do things to help the war effort, one thing I remember, we all had to collect books, paperbacks and magazines, these were supposed to be for the soldiers but when I think about it now, I don't suppose the soldiers had much time to read. I was quite good at drawing in those days, and one of my jobs was drawing posters to promote the things we were doing. Another thing the girls started was knitting. My nan had taught me to crochet, but I had never learned to knit, the knitting was supposed to help the war effort, but I really never knew how our little dish cloths were supposed to help.

We still went down to the air-raid shelter everytime the sirens went off. It started to get quite mad down there, I suppose there must have been about 300 of us, and to keep us quiet the headmaster used to take us for mental arithmetic, I really loved this, and to this day have always been able to add things in my head, it has stood me in good stead especially when shopping, when I get to the checkout I always know to the nearest pound what my bill is going to be.

As we proceeded to higher classes, our lessons changed. By the time I was eight years old we were starting to go to the domestic science classes, we were supposed to learn cooking but, because of the rationing, we were unable to do much of this, instead we learned how to do the washing. We had to take something from home to wash and iron. My mum usually gave a tea towel and one of my dads handkerchiefs (which she washed before she gave it to me). To this day, I still smilingly remember the effort that went into the soaking, scrubbing, rinsing and drying, then the ironing. We then proudly took our little laundry bundle home for mum and dad to admire. We had a little flat in one of the schools and we were taught to do housework. Always clear away any unused items, start from the top, dust the picture rails, dust the window frames, take up the rugs and put outside, sweep the floor and then dust all around. We were told that it was important to sweep before we dusted because, if you did it the other way around, the dust would settle again and you'd have dust all over again. We then shook and brushed the rugs and put them back on the floor.

Occasionally we were allowed to do some cooking, but this would depend if our parents could supply the ingredients, most of our cooking was with vegetables as these were the only things that were not rationed, I must admit I learned to make a lovely vegetable and lentil stew/soup, which my dad used to love.

LINE-UP FOR A DOSE OF MEDICINE

We also had sewing classes, again this was difficult because of the coupons, although the school was given a supply of very dull looking material, my project was a blouse, it took me a whole year to make, I got very good marks for my stitching, it was all done by hand but the material was so dull that it all seemed such a waste.

When I was eleven years old I sat for a scholarship to go to a higher school, as I was especially good at drawing and painting, my teacher thought I may gain by being at a better school, I won the scholarship, but unfortunately my parents couldn't afford the uniform and books that would have been needed so I missed that chance.

My schooling was interrupted by my frequent bouts of evacuation, but I always seemed to slip back into things again when I came back home. School dinners were started during the war, although I didn't have far to go I always liked to stay because we had afters, and at home we could only have afters on Sunday, we were also given a small bottle of milk and a spatula of malt, I really loved this, but I think it played quite a bit of havoc with my waistline, I was teased quite a bit by this time as I was getting a bit tubby, but my mum was always there to support me.

In 1945 after the war ended we were allowed to do more outdoor activities, I learned to swim, (something I still do on a daily basis), and we used to go to a gardens called *The Foundling*, where we could play rounders, netball and skipping.

The holidays always seemed so long, but when the war ended, we were able to go to the park more, our nearest park was Regents park, it had really lovely gardens and playgrounds. As I was older now, I used to take my little brother and his friends, and we would spend the whole day there, we never went away for holidays, our holiday was going to the hopfields, this always took place at the end of September, just as we were due to go back to school, so we had about nine weeks off in the summer. We were actually down the hopfields during the Battle of Britain, we watched the airplanes fighting and shooting. A German airplane came down in the fields near us, all the granddads and farm-hands surrounded him. When I think back, I don't know who was more scared, the pilot or our men, anyway, it wasn't long before the police came and took him away. I never knew what happened to him.

I was expecting to leave school in 1948 when I was 14. The new Labour government put paid to that. They raised the school leaving age to 15, it was to come into force on April 1st and as I was 14 on April 6th, I had to stay a whole year longer in school. That probably sounds as if it would have been a good thing for me, but I was the only child left in the class, all the rest of the leaving class had their birthdays before April 1st. As it was policy for each class to move up as the older class left, that left me with nowhere to go. I spent the rest of that year up until November helping to look after the infants. In the past there was a rota, each head girl would take it in turn, to help out once a week, but as there was nowhere for me to go, I became the permanent helper. My mum kept me home from school from time to time so that I could help her with her home work, this was hand sewing, which I was quite good at, the lady my mum worked for said she would give me a job when I left school as my sewing was so good, but my mum was always in hot water with the school board who came knocking on the door each time I was off school. Although my mum tried to reason with him that I was not learning anything at school, I still had to go back. In November, I spent all my time at school making the costumes for the school nativity play, so my mum's tuition with the needle was put to good use. After Christmas it was just a matter of biding my time to leave. My teacher tried to get me a job with a silk screen printing firm, but they said I was too young at 15. I eventually ended up working for the post office, I was learning to be a telephonist, but that is another story!!!'

PATRICIA TOS

ONE OF THE MOST SOUGHT-AFTER POSTERS FROM WWII

YORKIE'S STORY

Here are some recollections from 'Yorkie' of experiences that I have learned were shared by many:

'I was ten years old when WWII started. The first thing I remember is receiving a gas mask. This was a horrible smelly thing which covered all the face and went over the back of the head. I didn't feel that I could breathe in it. We had to carry this everywhere with us and it was in a square cardboard box with strings to carry over the shoulder. All the men in the street where I lived had to dig big holes in the garden and had to erect what were called 'Anderson Shelters'. Large corrugated sheets covered these contraptions and we had to go down a ladder to get inside where two double bunks were fitted for us to sleep on. These shelters always seemed to be very cold and damp. Once the air-raids commenced we had to use these shelters which were lit either with candles or kelly lamps.

At first we were still able to attend school where we regularly practised going down to the shelters if there was a raid during the day. I carried a box of biscuits in case we were down there a long time and got hungry. However, only months after the beginning of the war the schools where I lived closed and we had lessons in private houses. My father, who was 35 years of age in 1939 first became an air-raid precaution warden. Regularly after working during the day he went to the ARP post at night to be on call should there be an air-raid. If there was a raid he had to patrol the streets looking for incendiary bombs and if houses were bombed he had to help the people who were injured. Some houses were issued with stirrup pumps which were used to put out the fires. In the first air-raid I remember 'screaming' bombs were dropped and it sounded as though each bomb would directly hit the shelter where I was. This was very demoralising. In fact the bomb landed about half a mile away and did demolish two houses and people were killed. In 1940 my father was drafted into the army and at 36 years of age he found it hard to keep up with the 18 year olds doing the army exercises. It wasn't long before he was sent abroad.

SPECIALLY FOR D-DAY

At this time, my mother who had never been out to work since she was married, was forced to go to work in the munitions factories. It must have been very hard for mothers. Food became very short and we were issued with ration books. We received only very small rations of all the basic foods and eventually ate such things as reindeer meat, whale meat and something called snouk. They all seemed pretty inedible. My mother was a good cook and, when available, got marrow bones from the butchers with which she made soup with vegetables mostly grown in our garden. Fruit from abroad became non-existent and we didn't see a banana again until about 1951. I was lucky in that I had pen-friends in both Australia and America who often sent us food parcels. These often included wool and material as we were also given clothing coupons and therefore didn't get many new clothes.

When a parcel arrived we had a party because these usually contained tinned bacon, butter, dried eggs, meat and other delicious things which we were so short of.

Soon after the air-raids started my pen-friend's mother in Australia wrote to my mother to ask if she would like my brother and myself to be evacuated to live with them and my mother did agree, but by this time the evacuee ships were being bombed by the Germans so we never did go. Sheffield, where I lived, was a steel city and munitions were being produced in great quantities so, of course, Sheffield was a target for the German aeroplanes. We always thought we recognised the German aeroplanes by the throb of their engines. In the park across the road from where I lived a huge barrage balloon was erected which we could see from our windows. There was always great excitement with the children in the street when this managed to get away and in fact on one occasion a German plane set fire to it as it prevented the planes from making low-flying bombing runs.

Eventually schools were opened again and by this time I had passed the eleven-plus and had to travel to the other side of Sheffield to go to grammar school. My school was a new school which had only been open a year but unfortunately it had already been bombed when I started there. The most I remember about that school were the dreadful school dinners because of the shortage of food, so we never seemed to get anything nice.

Around the end of 1940 Sheffield was blitzed, but instead of bombing the steel works the centre of Sheffield was the target, and all the shops and pubs in the city centre were flattened, killing many people. The bomber seemed to have followed the trams along the tram tracks (probably due to them seeing the sparks from the tram tracks when they were moving) and so we were unable to travel about by tram for many weeks. Many of the big shops were flattened so it was hard to do any shopping for several months until shops were opened in the big houses, etc., on the edges of the city. Things were very makeshift. The restaurants and cafes, of which there were very few in those days, all had to close because of the shortage of food, but I do remember the 'civic cafes' which opened mostly for people who were at work and, as I remember it, we thought the food there was delicious.

I remember days after the town was blitzed my mother took my brother and me to the theatre to see Frankie Howerd. The theatre was almost empty and Frankie Howerd came on the stage to thank us all for coming and saying how brave we were. At this time the theatres and picture houses were still trying to carry on because, of course, we all needed a bit of cheering up, but if there was an air-raid an announcement came on the screen telling us and asking us to go to the nearest shelter. Large brick shelters were built in various places for the public to use if they were unable to get to their homes, otherwise, they went in the cellars of public houses or large stores and, as many of these large stores were bombed in Sheffield, many people sheltering in the cellars were killed. I also remember there were brick buildings in the parks which we heard were 'gas stations' where people who had been hit by gas bombs could go to be washed all over, but happily gas bombs were never dropped so far as I know.

As my father was now abroad we used to receive airmail letters from him which looked as though they were negatives of photographs as they were always in black and white. Most of the writing was blacked out and we never knew where my father was or if he was in any danger. He was unable to tell us anything about what was happening to him. There was always the constant worry that we would receive a telegram to say he had been wounded or killed as many of our neighbours and friends were receiving. Apart from all the other worries, my mother did not receive much army pay and so found it hard to pay for my bus fares and all the other things children need.

As the war progressed food became shorter and shorter and I remember that whenever the word got round that the butchers had received some extra rations such as sausages, liver, etc., or the sweet shop had received a supply of sweets or chocolate, everyone would rush to the shops and huge queues would form. Of course the extra rations didn't last long and many had to go home disappointed.

in a raid—

Motorists-park your car close to the kerb off the main highway. *AT NIGHT.* switch off head lamp. Keep side and rear lights on

AIR RAID ADVICE

By this time I was old enough to join the junior WAAF's with the idea that I would join up when I was old enough. I learned to march up and down. We had to learn about both our own and the German aeroplanes and we were occasionally taken to aerodromes to see how the RAF boys lived. We were taken to Bisley to see the anti-aircraft guns. All of which I found very grown-up and exciting.

At the end of 1944 we began having air-raids with 'buzz-bombs' and these were very frightening because first of all we could hear the throbbing of the engines chugging overhead and then when the throbbing noise stopped, the bomb fell, so you knew if you heard the engine stop the bomb would fall on or near you. London had been having these buzz-bombs for a while but we didn't think they would reach Sheffield. Then, we heard that they had invented an even more powerful unmanned flying bomb, but luckily I don't think any dropped on Sheffield.

The shortage of food and clothes got worse and worse and then the war ended and we waited for my father to come home. He was away from home for four and a half years and didn't seem to be the same as I remembered. He looked much older and greyer and it took us a long time to get used to each other again.'

YORKIE

JOIN UP!

ARTHUR'S STORY   LOCATION LONDON

'I joined the Metropolitan Police as a probationary constable in 1940, in the winter. I remember the day I got my uniform. It was the most expensive lot of stuff I had ever possessed. The coat was the warmest I had ever had and I needed it too. That first day I had it I went home and gave my mum a right fright. She thought it was someone bringing bad news, as my dad and uncle were in the navy and we were all worried about them.

The way we dealt with crime in those days was very strange at times. In the East End we had a lot of looting going on and so many burglaries. I was told to turn a blind eye to no end of things. For morale purposes I was told. But I was never happy about it. There was a lot of money made by the gangs in those days that helped establish some right old trouble after the war. Some of the biggest names of all got a good old leg-up from my superiors back then. I know that some of the coppers in my station were taking back-handers from the villains to turn a blind eye, because they certainly did a lot on a copper's money. It was not a good time to be in the force if you were straight. I met some of them after the war at a retirement party in the East End, I moved out of London in 1949 to another force, and they could hardly look me in the eye because they knew how corrupt they had been during the war. It may sound hard but I consider them to have been traitors of a kind as they did not do what they were being paid to do, keep people safe at a dangerous time.'

ARTHUR (EX-METROPOLITAN POLICE)

IF YOU ARE BOMBED OUT
and have no friends to go to

ask a
POLICEMAN
or your **WARDEN**
where to find your
REST CENTRE

A PLACE OF REFUGE
ESSENTIAL TO MANY

DON'S ACCOUNT   LOCATION BERKSHIRE

'I was eight years old at Christmas in 1943. The 'Yanks' gave us a
party in the 'Hut' East Hanney, Berkshire. They were 'D' Company
342nd Engineers USA Army and were camped at the Grove airstrip
just up the road.'

DON MCDOUGALL

A SOURCE OF
NOURISHMENT

DOT'S STORY LOCATION KENT

This is a verbatim account of a very hard life of work. The images Dot paints with her words are so vivid that I decided not to edit them in any way:

'In 1944 I was fourteen. I had no education. My education consisted of surviving school. I got my first job when I was thirteen and started it on my fourteenth birthday. I went to work in the steelworks in Scunthorpe in Lincolnshire, and I was still just a girl really and all I knew was the three R's. I could read a bit, I could write a bit and I could do arithmetic a bit.

So I started at Lycite Steelworks. My dad worked there, my brother worked there and we all worked with this foul stuff called… 'basic' which is a by-product of steel, it's the dust from the slag. I was what they called a 'barrow girl', you know like a porter's barrow, one of them, well there was, ooh, lots of us kids all fourteen, maybe some were 15, used to go to work at half past seven in the morning; we all got on the works bus in our overalls, you know the dungarees with your knapsack on your back with your bottle of cold tea and your baked bean sandwiches if you were lucky (if you weren't you had just bread and dripping, stuff like, uhmm… you know, you never had an apple or anything like that).

Anyway you get on this bus with all these other kids, half past seven in the morning, and then you got the bus at half past five at night to come home. Difference was when you come home you were covered in this dust. It was up your nasals. It was in your eyes. Your hair was stiff and black with it and it was all in the corners of your mouth. In your ear-holes, everywhere, wherever there was a hole it was in there. And of course when you got home there wasn't all this water that just come out of taps like in my home. You didn't, like, get in the bath, have a shower and wash your hair, or anything, you just give your hair a good brush. And before you went out that night to meet your mates you'd give yourself a good sloosh in a basin of water. Uuhmm… we got thirty bob a week and my dad used to give me half a crown; I was lucky really though, some of my mates had a bad time from their mams and dads.

Work? Blimey. If you can imagine this immense, a vast area, like a concrete area, and along side of it was like railway lines and these trucks, and in those trucks were two blokes because that's where my big brother worked, he was a loader. On t'other side there was the 'chute and, like, coming out of this air vent was this pipe coming from heaven with a big clip. The 'chute worker would put a sack on to this pipe, clip it on, pull a lever and all this hot stinking disgusting slag dust would fill this sack and then us barrow girls would come up with our barrow, hook it under this sack, undo the clip, pull it onto the barrow, run it down this concrete ramp. Oh, and sometimes the bloody sack used to fall off when it were half full and this stuff, the air was full of it; the sacks were made of hessian and the dust used to ooze out of them.

There was ten, twelve of us kids doing this. Yeah... thirty bob a week we got. I could pick one of these sacks up, but I couldn't carry it. Half-hundred-weight, fifty-six pounds I would say it weighed. We would line them up along this cement thing, then these older ladies, mature people, some of them nearly thirty years old. They would have these big needles on this string and they would hook through the top and you would finish up with like two ears on this sack. Then the barrow girls would come and pick one up and go to where there was a ramp up onto the side of the wagon and we pushed this barrow up this ramp and the bloke in the wagon would take it off onto his shoulder and he would stack them and when that wagon was full we'd go onto the next one. Day in; day out; all day; all week.'

Dot Baker continues her story with an account of her arrival in London, having escaped the unpleasant surroundings of the steelworks:

'I was still only 15 when I finally got out of the steel-works at Scunthorpe. I went to London to live with my sister. It was 1945 and the war was still on and it felt strange sitting in the dim light of a London bus in the blackout, no lights anywhere, just a tiny glimmer coming from the stairs that went down to the 'tube'.

By the time the war ended in September I was thoroughly enjoying myself – still 15, but I had a very full social life. Ballroom dancing was my passion, and my job as a shop-girl in Woolworth's was very much better than my job as a barrow girl, trundling half-hundred-weight bags of filthy slag-dust from 7.30 in the morning until 5 at night for 30 shillings a week.

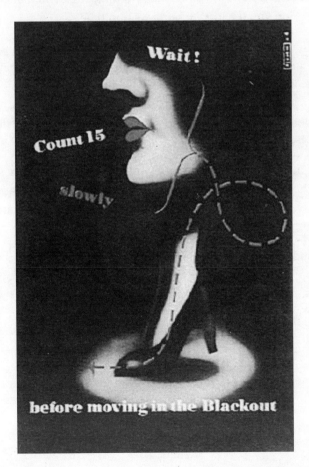

BE CAREFUL,
DON'T RUSH IN
THE BLACKOUT

We would go to the Putney Palais de Danse every Saturday, and there were lots of forces home on leave to dance with. I didn't take up with anyone special – just had a bloody good time! We had all got used to taking everything in our stride; young people's attitudes were very much 'enjoy yourself while you can, cos a doodlebug or a V2 can get you any time of the day or night'.

The lads on leave were certainly out for a good time and the Palais was where they went to have it. Not at all like today though – there was no bar for a start. At the interval we would all have cups of tea and a slice of cake. Socialising didn't mean getting tiddley, and being sober didn't stop you having a bloomin' good time.

Another difference was that we could walk back the couple of miles or so from Putney Palais at midnight without any fear at all. You would pass people, lots of people, sometimes a soldier or a sailor would say 'give us a kiss love' and you'd give him a kiss if you liked the look of him, but there was never any thought at all that you might suddenly be attacked by anybody.

Strangely, our determination to enjoy ourselves carried over past the end of the war, and looking back I can see that my generation considered war conditions to be 'normal' and we found it very hard to change our attitudes.

But all of a sudden we had all these soldiers and sailors coming back from the war, all wanting to get stuck in to a 'normal life' except that they wanted it to be different from what they had before the war. You know, a proper Health Service and such for a start.'

DOT BAKER (INTERVIEWED 3RD MAY, 1996)

CHRISTMAS COURTESY OF UNCLE SAM LOCATION NORFOLK

1944. A momentous year. The allies thrust, made that year, into Nazi Fortress Europe was to prove to be the fatal blow to Hitler's ambitions. On the home front the shortages were still a pain in the neck. Christmas was a time when these were felt more acutely.

CHRISTMAS IMAGERY MIXED WITH A TOUCH OF WAR

Here is a seasonal contribution from Eileen King:

'My Christmas in 1944 was really something special. My mum was involved with an American airman, a sergeant, called Andy Horton, stationed at Shipdham. That being the fourth Christmas of the war things were tight as there were lots of shortages. My brothers and sisters were not really expecting much.

Just before Christmas we had a knock on the door and it was Andy Horton. He had brought us a turkey that was so big we had to sit up all night to cook it in our shed in what is called a bread baking oven. That bird was glorious. Horton also made us a potato salad to go with it followed by peach pie.

We had things that Christmas that we had only dreamt of for so long. The piano in the front room was full of fruit, red rosy apples, oranges, sweets. There was a barrel of beer on bricks in the corner of the room. We had a really good Christmas. And so did our neighbours because my mum made sure she shared our good fortune.

TO ANSWER THE QUESTION: NOT MUCH!

There was a good supply of what Horton called 'firewater', which was in fact a very potent gin. My mother loved it. She had to have three weeks off work once because she had too much of the stuff. One morning we had a half a cup each before cycling to school. I don't know how we managed. I remember I could see three roads in front of me, so I just pointed my bike at the middle one. I must have looked a sight that morning.

When I was working at Metamec, in Dereham, I remember we used to stand on the roof of what was then called Moorgate House and watch the American Fortresses come home from their missions. Whenever those boys flew over they used to dip their wings to let us know they were coming. I can see the pictures on them now. There was Donald Duck, Betty Grable and the Four Leaf Clover was another.

Andy Horton sometimes used to come from Shipdham, drunk on his firewater, on his bike with a dozen eggs on the back and not one of them was broken. He knew how to handle his drink.

They were all nice boys, the Americans. In the summer they used to sit out in the garden and the neighbours up the road used to complain. I'd be indoors cooking chicken and the boys would be getting the old firewater down them. One of them, George Day, who went with my aunt Lena, was the cousin of the actress Lorraine Day who was well known then.

Then there was the story of the Spam. Andy Horton brought us some seven pound tins of Spam and the woman my family was living with threatened to report my mother for handling black market goods. So we had to dump it all in the local pit, the Neatherd Pit it was called and is still there, and so is the Spam probably. My brother Brian was angry we had to do that and boy did he swear. I can't possibly use the words he did.

Among my many memories of those days was the fact that my mum was the first person in our town to wear nylons.

They were marvellous times in a way. The Americans did all they could to help us and they were only young, a long way from home and a lot of them did not go back.

EILEEN KING

INSTANT SIBLINGS   `LOCATION HALIFAX`

Here are some memories of evacuees in the Northeast of England:

'I remember my mum telling me to get my coat on because there was a load of kiddies from London and we were going to get one. I was so excited. I didn't have any brothers or sisters and this was as close as I would ever get to one. (We lived in Warley Road, Halifax.)

My mum, Norah Hooson, was a 'no nonsense' type, small, about five feet tall, but feisty. I walked around the church hall and found a girl near to my age, a little older but then beggars can't be choosers. When my mum came over and told her we were going, she started to cry because she didn't want to leave her two sisters. My mum told them that as long as they didn't mind roughing it, she'd keep them all together. I remember Patsy and Joyce slept in the big bed with my mum and me and Maureen had the little bed. But they were all together and that was the most important thing.

Later the girls told mum about a friend that was being mistreated. That was enough to fire my mum up and it was 'Get ya coats on and let's get this kid NOW!!' off we went down Parkinson Lane, knocked on the door and I can hear my mum now. Ivy... get yer stuff, your coming with us, and that was that. We got an old mattress and Ivy Bridges. We had a lot of nothing but laughs.

I now live in America, but often wonder what happened to the Bygraves sisters... and do they wonder about Aunty Norah and Ann?'

ANN ECKROTH (NEE HOOSON)

PRESTON AT CHRISTMAS

FIRST CLASS SERVICE LOCATION SOMEWHERE IN ENGLAND

Here one Frank Foster recalls an interlude during a stopover at an RAF base. It is a classic example of how a personal recollection can summon up far off days to those who were not there:

'Returning from a mission in the Fall of 1944 in early evening on a fog bound night, we were short of gas and not certain of our position; we searched for any likely landing spot. At a very low altitude we passed a strip of concrete that appeared to be an acceptable solution to our problem. Following a sharp 360 degree turn we made an unapproved landing which ended with the plane coming to a halt abruptly at the end of a runway. An unfamiliar 'jeep' escorted us to a parking space where we were greeted by several British combat bomber crew members.

We were taken to the clubhouse where 'HIGH SPIRITS' were in hot demand. It appeared that every person in the bar demanded that he buy each of us a drink... glass after glass became a milk shake glass filled with booze... milkshake glass after milkshake glass continued... to the dismal distress of a potted plant in the bar which was the recipient of the contents of the milkshake glasses.

Then came dinner. We were served a hearty meal which included REAL EGGS. Apparently eggs were a real shortage in England and were served only to combat crews returning from a mission. (The American version of WWII eggs was a powdered version of a substance mentally described as an egg)... catsup use received a huge boost during this period.

Later we were deposited at a billet for the night. All was well as the billet was a very comfortable place with good furnishings. The next morning we were a bit surprised to be watching a female service gal (Wren) ironing our uniforms and polishing our shoes.

Our many attempts to convince our American superiors to adopt the 'in bed service' were never successful.'

FRANK FOSTER

DISCOURAGING THE
IMPORT OF FOODSTUFFS BY
VULNERABLE CARGO SHIPS

THE DEADLIEST RAILWAY LOCATION NORFOLK

I am grateful to the family of George Parnell for being so thoughtful as to write down his story. George was a good friend to me for many years and I know he would like me to ask that this following record of his experiences be considered an epitaph to his comrades with whom he shared them:

In 1940 George Parnell was sent to Scotland, then on to Northwich in Cheshire after which he sailed to Nova Scotia in Canada on October 14th 1941 before onward transportation to the West Indies, Capetown, South Africa and Mombassa, Kenya.

After Mombassa he sailed to India for a short time before being recalled to Mombassa again and transported to Singapore via the Maldives in the Indian Ocean; landing at Singapore on January 6th

1942. He was then in combat against the Japanese until February 15th 1942 when Singapore fell at 4.00pm.

George was taken prisoner by the Japanese and for six months he worked, with other prisoners of war, clearing the warehouses and docks at Singapore, living on rice and sweet potatoes. They were then moved up country to help construct the now infamous Burmese Railway, also known as 'The Railway of Death' because so many of the men died during its construction. George had no shoes and his clothes consisted of a 'Jap Happy' which was just a piece of cloth which went between their legs. When the railway was finished the prisoners went into the jungle cutting down trees for firewood which was fuel for the engines, as there was no coal. It was very hard work as temperatures rose to 120 degrees Fahrenheit in the shade. They were living on rice, salt and things like snakes and turtles and anything caught in the jungle. Because of the amount of rice, a ton and a half in all, along with husks and live maggots and beetles, he had to eat George vowed never to eat rice again after the war. He kept his vow.

Men were dying daily of starvation and diseases like cholera, beriberi and malaria etc. Sometimes as many as fourteen a day whose corpses had to be burned before the burial of the ashes in a ditch.

During the latter part of the war he was forced to cut sidings for the trains as the Japs were in retreat. On August 19th 1945, as a result of the atomic bombs being dropped on Hiroshima and Nagasaki, with terrible loss of life for the Japanese, they surrendered.

The prisoners came back down country through Thailand and the Air Force dropped food supplies for them on the way. Then they moved to Bangkok and flew to Rangoon for a few days before boarding a ship to sail home to England; arriving at Liverpool docks on October 11th 1945. They then took a train from Liverpool via Norwich to Dereham, in Norfolk. After they got demobbed at Ilfracombe in Devon they were given leave of absence to regain health and strength.'

COMPILED BY GEORGE'S FAMILY FROM HIS NOTES AND MEMORIES

SOME SAY THE WAR WAS WON ON THE MERITS OF DRINKING TEA

COURAGE UNDER FIRE   LOCATION NORTHUMBERLAND

'I am talking on behalf of my granddad and great uncle who are no longer alive, they both fought in the Second World War. My granddad John (Jack) Thwaite was in The Border Regiment. He landed in the assault wave on 'Gold Beach' on D-Day June 6th 1944, and my dad has told me about the terrible things he saw when they hit the beach that morning. He landed with 231 Inf Bde. He also fought in Caen and finally in Belgium where he was wounded while firing his Bren, he had been hit by either a German mortar or grenade, he went deaf in one ear and was virtually paralysed on one side, but he still held his ground and managed to lay fire down on the advancing Germans. He was then sent home because of wounds. My great uncle Lieutenant Tom Tarmey also landed on D-Day, leading his men off the landing craft onto 'Sword Beach'. He landed with the Northumberland Fusiliers. I don't know much more about Tom, but I do know he got to the Reichstag in Berlin in 1945, and actually found a piece of paper with Adolf Hitler's signature on it, which we have got at home.'

JAMES THWAITE

'EXCITING' TIMES   LOCATION SOMEWHERE IN ENGLAND

'I was a teenager when the war began and most persons of my age group found the war years exciting. People and forces were always on the move and we met so many people from all walks of life which we never would have done otherwise. I don't think we really understood the gravity of the situation.'

JEAN CEIROG-JONES (NEE REDMAN)

Heavy "Stirling" bombers raid the Nazi Baltic port of Lubeck and leave the docks ablaze

BACK THEM UP!

THE LINK BETWEEN THOSE BACK HOME AND THE AIRMEN
WAS ALWAYS SEEN TO BE STRONG

SWEET THINGS `LOCATION LONDON`

'I was born in London on Sept 11, 1940 during an air-raid, I don't have too many memories, I'm told I slept in a drawer under the bed! I do remember later going into the shelter and my father bringing me his chocolate bar ration from the RAF but my strongest memory is from after the war, the day rationing ended on sweets! I ran to the store only to find all the jars empty. Since then I have never let my sweet supply get too low!'

JENNIFER CRAIG (NEE GERRELLI)

A LESSON LEARNED `LOCATION MANCHESTER`

'I don't remember much about the war except seeing bombed houses that, to me, looked like dolls houses with the front exposed. I was curious about being able to look into other people's houses. I remember my family crying because an aunt had drowned on board the Athenia, which was the first ship to be torpedoed when war broke out in September 1939. I was born in September 1940 a year after war was declared and remember the grief of my family when discussing poor aunt Martha. She was on her way back home to Canada when the Athenia was fired upon. I can remember everyone saying how much like aunt Martha I looked. I saw a photo of her once and must admit there was a likeness. We lived in Church Lane, Moston, Manchester during the war and later lived in one of the new 'prefabs' at Heaton Park.'

JOAN PERKINS (NEE ALBISTON)

WE HAD NO BANANAS FOR YEARS LOCATION BIRMINGHAM

'I have a great interest in not allowing those times to be forgotten as even my own grown up family rarely ask about such times. Those war years had many stories to tell of hardships, sadness, pain and some humour as well. People were different then, I know we hear that so many times, but the fact is it is true. People shared and rallied each other and, as a child, we all had many mothers at those times, all mucking in together, all in the same 'mess'. The modern wars will always be different, but then everybody was kept in the dark about what was happening. All we knew then for certain was that we would scurry to our shelters at some unearthly hour of the night and listen to all those bangs and screams and crashes of the German bombs.

My grandfather was a Chief Air Raid Warden, and I can remember huddled in that dark damp shelter hearing this voice from beyond asking if everyone was alright, this before I was old enough to know he was my grandfather, he was just a voice in the dark.

My first banana. I couldn't say exactly when it was but certainly after the war ended and all the street parties of VE and VJ were over. My late mother gave us all this long soft yellow thing and said try these, but we didn't quite know what to do with them. When told they were for eating my younger sister took a bite out of hers, skin and all, spitting it out and saying 'it's nasty, I don't like it'. Then mother showed us how to peel them and all was revealed. I was told that there were flights during the war called 'banana baby flights'. These were special flights bringing bananas into Britain. Sounds far fetched doesn't it, but it appears that there have always been children whose lives were at risk if they didn't get bananas. (Something left over from our relationship to the apes I wonder?) But these children were called Banana Kids or Banana Babies and the flights were just to bring bananas in for them. I think my next memory of bananas was watching Johnny Weissmuller 'Tarzan' on the Saturday Matinees feed bananas to his chimp. Happy days.'

JOHN DAVIES

DRIVING IN THE WAR
NEEDED A NEW SET
OF RULES

TRADERS IN THE DARK MARKET   LOCATION LONDON

Even after so many years have passed it is still relatively rare to find anyone willing to discuss the Black Market in anything other than the sketchiest terms. This contribution from Jim Wilcox is therefore most welcome:

'Well, I don't know if I should say this or not… but over 60 years on I guess it doesn't matter much any more. My parents were in business in London and naturally had many business contacts. One of these people owned a farm in Barnet, which at that time was just outside London but is probably well within London's boundaries today. We were one of the few people with a car, a 1936 Morris Oxford, which incidentally no-one except my Navy uncle could drive at that time, and since he was at sea for a good part of the war and petrol was rationed it probably qualified as one of the lowest-mileage cars ever. However, when he was home we used to drive to this farm, other times we simply took the bus and tube.

The farmer would phone us whenever he had a government allocation to slaughter some pigs and we would go there and buy a fair amount of pork and bacon, but couldn't take all he wanted to sell since there was no such thing as refrigerators in the houses. We had eight people to feed, (grandmother, my mum and dad, my brother, me, one uncle and two aunts all living in the same house) so I imagine we still purchased a fair amount. He also had eggs and beef for sale which we bought, but of course the prices for all this Black Market stuff were exorbitant as he certainly didn't lack customers. Rationing was so harsh that anyone who had connections and could afford to buy food on the Black Market did so, especially if they had children. Practically everything was available on the Black Market in the 1940's, in fact rather well-dressed men who were known as 'Spivs' or 'Wide Boys' would stop you on the street and offer cigarettes, tobacco, beer, watches, canned food staples, nylon stockings, chocolate and just about anything providing you had the money to pay for it. The sporty clothes and expensive suits and spats were a sort of 'trademark' which identified these people to everyone.

I am in no doubt a lot of money was made, but I had no idea of their sources of these goods. Some of it was no doubt salvaged from bombed warehouses and ships docked in the harbours. In fact I can remember getting 'distressed' tins of jam, again, at a price. Much of it I'm sure was simply stolen goods. Probably much of it came from American army bases, as the Americans seemed to have everything in abundance and I distinctly remember buying American cigarettes for my dad – who wouldn't smoke them. His brand was Craven 'A' and he would smoke nothing else.

As far as who operated the Black Market is concerned I'm afraid I have no idea. There was probably some organisation to it on a country-wide scale, but as far as I knew it was ordinary people like the farmer who had access to surplus goods and sold them for whatever price they could get. People really were hungry a lot of the time and I hope never to see those days again.'

JIM WILCOX

DISCOURAGING THE AMERICAN BLACK MARKET

ARNHEM: NOT A MEMORY TOO FAR `LOCATION BIRMINGHAM`

'In September 2000 I visited Arnhem. As one of the last of the National Service Conscripts to the RAF those brave men gave me so much stick during the week there. I revelled in the fact that I was among those few that are left, and I learned so much from them. But their leg pulling was the usual servicemen's taunts, which stemmed very much from the fact that it was my lot that took those men in. But standing at the graves of so many men I felt so very insignificant, then two or three of them came and took me to the graves of some of Transport Command's dead. At that point we were, in their words not mine, 'equal in our life'. I had served whether in peacetime or war, I had served, and I felt so proud to be with all these lovely people.

The last evening there they repaid the leg pulling with so much fun that I ached with laughter. Then they all, every single one of them, came over and thanked me for being there with them. Yet I felt it an honour, my father had drummed Arnhem into me as a young man and I had finally made it to that place of death and glory, it was one of the most wonderful weeks of my life. It is a pity some of the younger people do not involve themselves more and go there. To see all the local Arnhem children, who tend those war graves for one year of their lives, is a beautifully moving sight to behold.'

JOHN DAVIES

NEVER GLORIFY WAR `LOCATION SOMEWHERE IN ENGLAND`

From John Phillips a most succinct contribution worthy of attention:

'I would now like to dedicate this entry to all of those contributors who expressed their appreciations for the efforts given by ordinary folk like me during the hostilities of the 1940 era, whether they were civilians or service personnel. To our young readers I would say 'never glorify war or regret that you were not a participant'. Having written my personal memoirs for my children and grandchildren I still vividly recall the austerities, fear and horror of those times both as a civilian and in 1942 a serviceman. I also remember with equal clarity the *'Esprit de Corps'*, camaraderie, and neighbourliness shown by the ordinary folk of that era. At 80 years I now regret that the latter does not exist today.'

JOHN PHILLIPS

HELPING YOUR NEIGHBOUR WORK BY CARING FOR THEIR CHILDREN

BOMBED OUT IN THE LONDON BLITZ LOCATION LONDON

'My name is Kathleen Brockington. I married my husband in June 1939 at the age of 23 and can remember clearly that day in September hearing the Prime Minister tell us on the wireless that war had started.

For the first few days a lot of people were very frightened. I can remember my mother-in-law bursting into tears and putting her gas mask on that first day; she wore it for about an hour but nothing happened and she took it off again when we gave her a cup of tea and she realised she couldn't drink it with the gas mask on!

INSTANCES OF LOOTING OFTEN FOLLOWED AN AIR-RAID

In 1940 the air-raids started up proper. Like lots of others down our street we had an Anderson Shelter in our garden, but it was dreadfully damp so in the end we used to sleep under our big oak table. If the air-raid sirens went off in the evening we would just ignore them and carry on eating our tea or playing cards until we heard bombs getting a bit close, and then we would dive under the table for cover. (Maybe I should explain that we lived in Acton near where the Rolls Royce factory made the armoured cars and the bombers were always trying to get it).

The night I was bombed out my husband was away fire-fighting around St Paul's Cathedral and the East End of London which was getting a proper pasting. Lots of people were sleeping in the tube (underground railway) after the last train had gone.

When the bomb dropped I wasn't even under the table! I heard the plane and recognised it was a Jerry (that's what we called them) because I'd heard so many. There was a tremendous BANG! and I ducked. All the windows came in and the ceiling and a couple of walls came in, and there was incredible smoke everywhere. I was shaking like a leaf but I wasn't hurt.

I tried to get out but the door was stuck and I had to climb through where one of the windows had been. I could see there were lots of houses affected, glass everywhere in the street so I knew it was a big'un.

I ran to the Air Raid Post but the Warden said 'look missus, we're gonna be busy digging bodies out, if you've got a roof you're better off where you are. There's lots worse off than you'. Funnily enough he was wrong; about 50 houses were badly damaged and a couple of them just turned into heaps of rubble, but nobody was actually killed.

I went home and climbed back through the window. There was dust and glass and bricks everywhere but I slept on my bed in my clothes until 6am, then went to stay with my mother. I was very shocked of course, and worried that when my husband got back from working day and night putting out fires he would go home and assume the worst. One of my mum's neighbours had a telephone and I tried to find out where he was but around the East End of London it was a proper mess and nobody knew anything.

After a few months the house was patched up by a local firm (the government paid for that) so I could live in it. A right shoddy job they made of it too. When they finished there were still big cracks in the walls, bare pipes, dust and dirt everywhere for weeks on end; but like the wardens said, there were lots worse off and at least I was still alive.'

KATH BROCKINGTON

A RARE PHOTOGRAPH OF AN 'OP'S ROOM' PLOTTING TABLE IN USE

FATE: THE HAND OF THE GODS   LOCATION KENT

Here is a story that shows how fickle fate can be, and how in war things can pivot upon the success or failure of military planning:

'My dad was a railwayman in Kent. We were a real railway family. My granddad and great granddad were all railwaymen and steam was in our blood. I used to like to go to the station and watch all the trains and the soldiers loading them up. We used to watch as they loaded all the stuff for the big guns on the coast. I remember one day in 1942, it was Halloween I think, the Germans attacked the Folkestone to Canterbury line. I used to have the newspaper my mum kept with the story, but I lost it during a move in 1957. It was a terrible thing to do as it killed the little boy of a friend of my dad's. He wasn't supposed to have been on it as it was carrying military supplies as best as I can remember. I was only seven at the time so don't remember it very well. My dad told me later, after the war, that on the day before that attack prime minister Churchill had been on the train with President Roosevelt. They had been on their way to a parade or some such. My dad was always wondering if the raid had been intended for that train rather than the one that was hit. And if it was, whether someone he knew had been a German spy. There were several people he was suspicious of. He never said but I think he may have told the police about one man who left the district not long afterwards.'

LENNY

LETS HEAR IT FOR HARRY LOCATION GLOUCESTERSHIRE

This is the story of how Leonard Page came to end up at Chapel House in Chipping Norton, staying with Harry Knight and family, as an evacuee throughout the war:

'I was eight and three quarters when with haversack, gas mask, a pack of sandwiches and some sticks of barley sugar to give us strength mum said, my twin sisters Win and Doll were sent to Glengal Road School with me tagging along to be evacuated, the big experience, the unknown. We were lined up in the playground in groups supervised by teachers.

There were two or three days false start when transport did not turn up to take us away, of course this did not stop us eating the barley sugar as soon as we got to school 'to keep our strength up'.

Finally we departed with much waving, shouting and tears from the mothers who did not see it as the adventure we thought it was. Mum's strict orders were that the twins and me were to keep together, which we did, when we finally arrived at our destination it was dark and I can't remember much about the journey to Eynsham which was seven miles from Oxford. We were taken to the school hall where we stood around waiting to be picked, somewhat like a cattle market. A lady that wanted two girls picked my twin sisters, while myself and another boy, who came from the Isle of Dogs, named Kenny Gordon were picked by a couple who wanted two boys. My sisters, who remembered that mum said we must stay together, were in tears at us being parted but were finally subdued when told we would be living opposite each other in Mill Street, and so we parted.

But the excitement for me was far from over on being led out by Mr and Mrs Coates to a car, my first car ride made it seem worth leaving London for.

When we arrived we were told that we were to live on a farm, 'Home Farm' it was called. The house seemed massive after two up, two down and a basement scullery. There was kitchen, dining room, gun and billiards room with a full-sized table, a bathroom and toilet with bedrooms on the first floor and further upstairs was the attic room (one to be mine and Kenny Gordon's, with a bed of our own each).

That evening we sat down to dinner at an enormous table with about a dozen people who were guests and the farmer Mr Coates (whose wife always called him 'Hubby') began to carve a huge piece of meat. I was asked if I wanted ham and I said yes because everybody else who had been asked had said yes. Another first, a slice of ham that nearly covered the plate, with the maid bringing in vegetables in dishes from the kitchen. It seemed a strange way to have dinner, our mum always put everything on your plate before giving it to you.

AHHHHHH...

It was quite a big farm but we were soon exploring and finding our way about. We had to attend the local school with teachers who had been evacuated with us. I had a new teacher who when filling out the register asked my name, Len Page said I, 'Is Len short for Leonard' she asked, no my name is Len, no it can't be its Leonard, no I insisted its Len, no one in my life had called me Leonard (I could not remember my Christening). Anyway another first, for me, learning how to spell my own name, how could a boy of nearly nine expect to find an 'O' in his name, also come to terms that Leonard was my real name, fortunately everyone continued to call me Len.

I remember one thing that happened when the Scouts, whose ranks had been swelled by Londoners, came to collect waste paper for the war effort. We had been sent to show them where it had been stored in the barn, seeing as most of the scouts were known to me being in the top classes from school and also Islanders from the Isle of Dogs I also showed them where the apples were being stored in the loft of the barn.

"Hi—what about a comma or something after my name?"

UNDER-COUNTER
SALES WERE OFTEN A
SOURCE OF HUMOUR

I'm not sure whether apples or waste paper were the most to leave the barn that day but Kenny told Mrs Coates what I had done. From then on I was in the doghouse with her, although I got on very well with the farmer. At one time they expected bombing so Ken and I had to sleep in a downstairs room on a mattress on the floor with a hot water bottle between us which had a double purpose, one – to keep the bed warm, two – it still being warm in the mornings the water was used for washing in, so saving fuel heating washing water. One night I woke up in the dark wanting a wee but the house being in darkness I was frightened to try to find the bathroom upstairs. When I couldn't hold on any longer I opened the water bottle and topped it up, next morning I was quite happy to wash in cold water, this is the first time I have ever told this secret but it makes me think, if Kenny has a good complexion he can thank me, if he hasn't it serves him right for telling on me about the apples!

My dad came down to see us about Christmas time with tons of presents for the twins and me but they were not to be opened until Christmas day. Our mum could not come to see us because she was an invalid but her love came with dad. Dad always impressed me because he always called the farmer Gunner when he spoke to him, but in later life I found out he called any stranger Gunner.

Sundays big event was to go to Church and watch the army marching to and fro because they always sung as they marched. I do not know what regiment it was but they sang 'They didn't know chalk from cheese'. After Easter in 1940, because nothing was happening, mum had us home until there was another scare and we were evacuated for a second time.

Once again with haversack and gas mask and stick of barley sugar we went, this time, to Chipping Norton, which is 20 miles from Oxford. I remember less about the trip to Chippy than the first time we went to Eynsham, but after the train stopped off at other stations along the way dropping off parties of children we finally arrived and were taken to the town hall for distribution. This time my sisters and I, with the three Wise sisters, were taken to Chapel House, it consisted of a farm and seven cottages on one side of the road and the White House, a big house in its own grounds with another cottage which was for the White House workman on the other side of the road.

The Wise sisters were sent to the White House cottage, my sisters went to number 6 with a Mr and Mrs Powers and their son Puffy whilst I went next door to number 7 Chapel House. I lived with Mr and Mrs Knight (Harry and Ada) and their son Dennis who was only ever known as Sam. Since late 1940 when I arrived I have kept in touch with the Knights. Mrs Knight died in 1972 and dear old Harry died in May 1987 aged 89 years. Fortunately I went to see him three weeks before he passed away after a short illness. By now he lived in an old people's home at Bicester, near his now married son Sam and wife Doris. During this visit as usual we talked about the war years when I stayed with them. I always thought of him as my second dad and although I never got round to calling him Harry, I don't think I could ever show more respect than calling him Mr Knight. Harry had been a Grenadier Guardsman in the First World War, when volunteering at the age of fifteen, after walking twenty miles to the Oxford recruiting office, the recruiting Sgt. told him he was too young to join up and to come back when he was sixteen, which was what he did. He walked round the block and this time when the same recruiting Sgt. asked his age he said sixteen and was signed up. He received bad leg injuries in France and was invalided out with honours.

When I arrived at Chippy Harry was a wartime special policeman, but before the war ended he had joined or transferred to the fire brigade near London.

Harry and I would talk of how near Christmas time Mrs Knight had made a special cake to be iced for the festivities, Sam had asked his mum for a piece of cake and I was told to cut him a piece, there were two cake tins, the wrong tin was opened and a large lump cut out of what should have been the special Christmas cake. As Harry said 'The missus cussed you boy' the one and only time she did, although

Sam and I together gave her plenty of reasons to cuss us. Ada was a constant puffer of fags and loved whist drives, she always boasted that she had never had to buy a chicken for Christmas dinner, she always won one at the whist drive. If Ada was without fags due to shortages she would resort to rolling Harry's pipe tobacco in newspaper to have a puff.

ONE OF THE COLDEST JOBS: PICKING SPROUTS

Evacuees were not as plentiful in Chippy as they were in Eynsham so the Londoners were easily integrated with the other school children, and soon I was talking like the 'Carrot Crunchers', with plenty of sun and fresh air, helping at hay-making time in the fields of Hartley's farm during the school holidays, for this was the time of double summer time when it was still light at bedtime. Chapel House might not have been as grand as Home Farm, the bath was a tin one in front of the living room fire once a week. The toilet was outside, no flush cistern, but a bucket which Mr Knight emptied once a week and buried in a trench in the allotment, you never saw him empty the bucket and only knew it had been emptied by the large cabbage leaves that lined the bottom of the bucket! When I returned to London it took quite a time (and reminders) to learn to pull the chain again. The memories of Chipping Norton seem vaguer than the early part of the war but I think this is because I was one of the family rather than staying **with** a family. One highlight at Chippy was when a bomb was dropped near a pig farm at the bottom of Green Lanes about a mile and a half from Chapel House, and I think that every child in Chippy made the pilgrimage to see the crater the bomb had left.

I remember on Maundy Thursday, Sam and I walked to Over Norton to receive bread issued from the village hall to people who lived within the parish. My great delight at Chapel House was when I received a card from Chippy station to collect a parcel, the parcel was a full size bike which had belonged to my sister May who was still in London, although she did come and stay next door with the twins during some of the worst bombing in London. That bike was the best present ever, for no more the mile and a quarter walk to school, also when Mrs Knight went to the whist drive, Sam who was four years younger than me rode on the rear carrier of the bike while I walked or trotted behind. Sometimes it was a source of revenue as one boy at school would give me three pence to ride it about for the school dinner time. But this came to a stop when Mr Knight who was on point duty outside the town hall caught the boy on my bike (it being a girls sports bike) and he thought he had pinched it!

The war for some who were lucky like me, as much as we missed our parents, received as much love and attention as being at home.

Whenever I saw Mr Knight he always introduced me to his friends as 'My little evacuee from London.' Thanks Harry.'

LEONARD PAGE

CARING FOR CHILDREN AROUND
ENGLAND LOCATION SOUTH COAST AND LONDON

Evacuation was a logistic nightmare. So many children to be moved in highly abnormal conditions. Mary Langley worked as a 'Journey Nurse' and her story goes some way to add detail to the subject of evacuation:

'During the war I worked at County Hall three days on and three days off. I worked with evacuees as a 'Journey Nurse', picking up children who were not happy or who were disabled, and taking them to safety. There would be expectant mothers as well.

A SERVICE
WHICH TOOK AN
EMOTIONAL TOLL

FIRST TO HELP

The Red Cross in Action

QUICK, skilled action may save a life—your life perhaps, your wife's, your child's.
A trained army, 275,000 strong, ceaselessly at work in convalescent homes, air-raid shelters, first-aid posts, sick bays or with the V.A.D.'s in military hospitals—that is one among the many contributions which the British Red Cross and the Order of St. John are making towards victory. It is work that must go on. It is work that needs money. Send every penny you can spare to:

THE DUKE OF GLOUCESTER'S

RED CROSS & ST. JOHN FUND

ST. JAMES'S PALACE, LONDON, S.W.1

Issued by the War Organization of the British Red Cross Society and Order of St. John of Jerusalem. (Registered under the War Charities Act, 1940.)

AN INVITATION TO DONATE MUCH NEEDED FUNDS

In September 1939, I had taken part in a practice evacuation by bus with 62 children. We ended up in Dymchurch on the south coast of England and stayed there until the following May. These were disabled children who had previously lived at home. Very soon the authorities realised that being on the coast put us at some danger from enemy planes so we were moved inland to Oxfordshire.

Where we were staying there were no air-raid shelters, which meant that if there was an air-raid they got under their beds (which wasn't always easy with some of the children who were physically handicapped).

I also worked in various stately homes and large mansions around the country which had been given by their owners for use with evacuees. I remember one very splendid country house where the children all slept in the ballroom, as many as seven to a bed – sideways on – while Lord and Lady so-and-so lived in a couple of rooms in a different wing. We brought in our own cooks and employed house-mothers from London residential schools.

PULLING THE AMERICAN
PATRIOTIC HEART
STRINGS TO RECRUIT
MORE NURSES

Very early on I applied to be a nurse. I was only 19 and couldn't have general training until I was 21 but I was told I could be a 'fever nurse'. The funny thing is that when I got to 21 they said I wasn't tall enough (I had to be 5'3') so I couldn't be a general nurse. That was in London; provincial hospitals weren't so fussy so I did my training in Northampton and was there for 4 years.'

A NURSE UNDER THE BOMBS

Mary Langley tells us more of her war. As a nurse she was at times obliged to work in harms way, and for pitiful pay. Here an account of a day in the Blitz:

'I worked in London and I can remember one particularly bad 24 hours. I was at County Hall, right opposite the Houses of Parliament and had just been delivering some disabled children to the coast. I lived in Earl's Court in a flat. There was no air-raid shelter in the house and we usually just sat under the kitchen table when the bombers were close.

During the day we took no notice of sirens but when they blew whistles it meant 'imminent danger' and then we would take cover. One evening we had an air-raid warning and later that night I heard whistles – that meant pulling on some clothes and getting under the kitchen table again – but we were quite jolly and well used to that. We heard all the ack-ack guns going off in Hyde Park and Kensington Gardens and when I looked out I saw that search-lights had picked up some bombers just above the barrage balloons that covered all of London during those years.

Suddenly a warden knocked on our door and told us to get out quick – we took this sort of thing all in our stride, since I was still partly dressed anyway I ran, still with my slippers on, to the deep shelter under Earls Court Exhibition Hall. This was 40 feet down and fairly safe unless it got a direct hit, so I joined the 200 or so people already there. There was lots of talking and the usual singing (real cockneys always loved to sing during the air-raids – they could always be relied upon to keep cheerful).

I had insisted on getting into my nurses uniform so I would be able to help if needed but still had my slippers on. In the morning we were told not to go back because some 'oil bombs' had dropped in the area so I borrowed my landlady's shoes – they were a tight fit but at least I looked respectable.

That day there were no less than seven 'imminent dangers' each of which meant I had to run down three flights of stairs and into the basement shelter everytime, still in these shoes that were far too small. By the end of the day my feet were killing me!

Fortunately I was prepared for this sort of thing and always had a fiver safety-pinned into my vest, so I rushed out and bought a pair of shoes.

We were never allowed back to live in the Warwick Road flat because of the oil bombs which had gone off that afternoon. I was only allowed back to get a few things.'

MARY LANGLEY

LONDON UNDER THE BOMBS   LOCATION LONDON

'I live now, in 1995, where I've lived all my life. It's around the Goldhawk Road, Shepherds Bush, in West London.

As a young schoolgirl I can remember walking home with my friend Ruby to find that Askew Road (where Ruby lived) was roped off by the Air Raid Wardens because there was an unexploded bomb in one of the gardens. She came on home with me and there was her mum having a cup of tea at my house still a bit shocked and covered with earth because the bomb had fallen into the garden just a few feet from her and showered her with lumps of dirt!

Ruby and I were dead keen to see a bomb, so we rushed off and ducked under the barrier (nobody spotted us or tried to stop us) and went and had a good look at it. I can remember being amazed at the size of it, and it had fins sticking up just like in the pictures.

Looking back I suppose I should have been scared, but it's a fact that you can't live your life with your knees knocking all the time and in the end you just get on with it.

One time I felt really upset was when I was at the cinema and there was an air-raid (they put a slide up to tell you in case you wanted to go to a shelter, but hardly anybody ever did... if the bombing got close the roof-spotters would come down and tell you and then you might go out).

Anyway, when we got out after the film everyone was standing looking at the red sky over the London Docks – about 8 or 10 miles away from us, but burning, burning like I'd never seen before, so that the whole sky was lit up. It shook my mum a bit seeing that, and it made me thank my lucky stars I didn't live in the East End.'

ROSA NEWBY

MONKHOUSE IN THE DOGHOUSE LOCATION SOUTH COAST

THE LATE COMEDIAN AND
TELEVISION PRESENTER
BOB MONKHOUSE

A dramatic account of action on the Home Front is fondly recalled by the late comedian Bob Monkhouse, whose story begins when he was 11:

'Just before the end of August 1939, my father stood up after Sunday lunch in our Beckenham home and announced that Hitler was sure to launch a massive surprise blitzkrieg upon London. He told us that he had bought a small house in West Worthing and that we were to move down there at once.

During the phoney war, that strangely peaceful period that followed the declaration of hostilities, I wondered if my father had been right to move us to the south coast. His prediction of the London Blitz wasn't happening, but every Worthing lamp-post had placards exhorting residents to 'Stay Put'. The inference drawn was of invasion and people were beginning to talk of extended holidays in Scotland and Eire.

One sunny morning in the following July, the distant pulsing growl of a plane engine made me look up at the sky to see a (German) Dornier

17 bomber flying very low and slowly over the rooftops, heading towards me. The German plane passed directly over my head leaving a sooty trail. I could see the outline of a pilot's helmet as the aircraft swept away and a few moments later I smelt the oily odour of the smoke. Two Spitfires came banking down from over the sea, engines grinding out a lighter note than the bomber. Immediately behind them, higher and in a V formation three Me-109s appeared like shepherds searching for their lost sheep. All the planes vanished inland and then, lower than ever and with its right engine flickering with little rosy petals of flame, the Dornier returned, heading for the sea. One of the crew of four was pressed against a glass panel in the bulging forward section and I saw something fall as the pencil-shaped body of the fuselage glided away.

The RAF and German fighter planes were scribbling angry patterns in the blue high above and the angry chatter of their guns was surprisingly loud. By this time, I was on my bike, cycling as fast as I could round the little lanes to see if I could find what had fallen from the Luftwaffe bomber. Lots of people were out of their houses, shielding their eyes as they gazed upwards. My gaze was downwards. When I saw it lying in the gravel at the edge of a private drive, I recognised it at once. It was a military mess tin, a grey metal box with a lid, intended to carry rations. It was stamped with the outline of a swastika on one side and a spread eagle on the other. Inside it were three photographs, a coloured stone and a letter in German on yellow paper. The photos showed a handsome young man with close-cropped hair and wearing an NCO's uniform jacket, a pretty young woman posing coyly beside a farm pump, and a fat baby on a rug in a bushy garden.

I later heard that the Dornier had hit the sea and broken up about two miles offshore. There had been no survivors. Alone in my room at night I pored over the letter. It seemed to be addressed to someone called Fremde, which I took to be the name of the girl in the photo. I could picture the desperate airman, resigned to a fatal crash, hastily penning his last message of love to his young wife in Germany and then casting it from his dying craft.'

Monkhouse couldn't read German but his teacher at the nearby Goring Hall School, Mr Hatfield, could. To avoid any possible confiscation of the letter the youngster struggled to copy it, giving the freshly written one to his teacher.

On returning home after school, the young lad was met, not greeted, by his mother, who was terribly enraged, and by the headmaster, Mr Green. Monkhouse was quizzed about how and where he found the note, and was subsequently sent to bed without his supper.

It transpired that the letter was encouraging sabotage of the British war effort. The photographs were typical examples of healthy strong and friendly German people.

The stone, however, was a valuable piece of red jasper dating back to Roman times, intended to fund the cost of derailing trains and starting fires. Monkhouse recalled, 'I was given to understand that the gem had been surrendered to the Crown. I didn't much care. All I knew was I had a month of extra prep, early bedtime and not going to the Worthing Odeon. Bloody Jerries!'

TEATIME FOR TOMMY – *HOME FROM SCHOOL IN 1942*

ORANGES AND RUMOURS OF ORANGES LOCATION LONDON

'It's the year 1942 and I'm 9 years old, walking the familiar half-mile from school to my home in southwest London. Today was an ordinary day – I had my free bottle of milk at playtime and still had time to go out and play 'Spitfires and *Messerschmidts*' with my mates afterwards. It wasn't a day when I had to line up for a spoonful of VIROL – a sticky extract of malt we have to swallow once a week (which some of us like but which makes Billy Fletcher feel sick, but I think he's just a weedy type).

As I walk past the fruit and vegetable barrows in the High Street, I check to see if there are any orange boxes hidden under the barrows. My mum heard a rumour that a ship had arrived at Liverpool with a cargo of oranges, and because of my baby sister we've got a Green Ration Book, which means we might get one or two if there are any — but there aren't. Maybe the ship that was bringing them got caught by U-boats in the Atlantic.

"These simple things..."

In the quiet of the evening, waiting perhaps for the nine o'clock news. All that is peaceful and restful is centred in the room, around the fireside.

Such simple ordinary things—a thrilling book, a special chair, the favourite, homely nightcap—OXO.

These are the things that make up home.

PREPARED FROM PRIME RICH BEEF

THE 'IDEAL' FIRESIDE, VERY MUCH OF ITS TIME

Once home I tuck into my usual tea of bread-and-margarine. This stuff has very little colour and tastes more like grease, and not at all like butter! I know there's some butter in the cupboard (ordinary people don't have a refrigerator, only Americans and rich people have those) but that's special. I would really, really like some dripping on my bread (that's the fat that collects in the roasting pan when we have meat. It goes hard and you spread it on your bread and it's absolutely wizard!) but my mum's saving up the dripping.

The jam ration is nearly gone so I have to spread it on my bread-and-marge very thinly – just the merest smear. There's a pot of Parsnip Jam we got 'off-ration' but it isn't very nice and I prefer to eat what I've got. Bread isn't rationed so I eat about six slices. That will keep me going until 8, when I get a snack of cheese on toast with a cup of hot Oxo.

Tomorrow we'll have one of our favourite meals… roast potatoes (that's why I'm not allowed the dripping) and boiled cabbage with a 'knuckle' of bacon boiled with the cabbage. I may even get a slice of bacon too!

Yes, on the whole we're OK. We don't live like the King and Queen and Princess Elizabeth in the Palace, but we're healthy and alive and maybe on Saturday I'll get an extra boiled egg! (One a week for grown-ups but two for a Green Ration Book).'

TOM HOLLOWAY

IN THE TRENCHES LOCATION NORTHEAST

'I was born in 1932 and saw the raids on Tees-side. One bomb fell in our school playing field (Hartburn School). The first few weeks of the war we spent a lot of time in mud trenches with corrugated steel sheets as roofs in that playing field.'

PETER WILKINSON

100 BATHS A DAY LOCATION SOUTH COAST AND LONDON

'I suppose everyone has a bath now, but it wasn't so in the poorer parts of London in those days. So one of my jobs was taking groups of 20 children to the public (warm) baths in Walham Green, five groups every day, 100 children in all. If there are any mothers reading this perhaps they would like to imagine the fun I had giving 100 baths a day!

I saw plenty of examples of head-lice, body-lice and even scabies in those difficult days, although the rations we got were wholesome enough and children were generally healthy and active. Parents had to give permission for their children to be given a bath if we found any children especially verminous and not all parents co-operated. This meant I had to get a '149 Exclusion Notice' from the County to have children de-loused and cleaned or they would be excluded from school.'

MARY LANGLEY

OLD MEMORIES DIE
VERY HARD   LOCATION SOMEWHERE IN ENGLAND

This contribution is very evocative, however, it is not a point of view that is rare among those I have interviewed:

'From my point of view the Germans started WW1 and lost it and then had to pay the cost of their folly. Once again they decided to hold the world to ransom with WW2 and failed again. The Germans seem to have a fixed idea that they can go where they want and take property belonging to others, and change the laws of the countries they steal from. They hang people, gas them, poison them, then when caught they expect to be treated like they have done no wrong and some are still arrogant enough to try to argue they were in the right. But when the boot is on the other foot they whinge that they are not being properly treated. The U.K. was bombed by Germany for four years. Dresden was bombed for a couple of nights and some are even now whingeing that the R.A.F. should not have done it. Goebels was screaming for total war and he got it. Let us have no more stupid remarks that the R.A.F. should not have bombed Germany as they did. I think they deserve every praise and the people who are now deriding them should be made to suffer the same conditions that we had to put up with as POW for four years. I tried to escape from Salonica POW camp in Greece. Myself and another chap were beaten by the SS to the point of death when we were caught and ten Greek civilians were put up against the wall and shot. One was an 80 year old woman another was a twelve year old boy. The other man who was beaten died, I was fortunate in that some lads scrounging for food found me in a disused barrack room covered in bed bugs and they smuggled me onto the train that took us to Germany and a POW camp. I understood that the Americans in charge of rations for the German POW doled out the same meagre amount the Germans had been feeding the American POW in German hands. I often read things where Germans say 'the British could not manage to beat us on their own', I notice the Germans also had assistance from Dutch sympathisers, King Boris, the Japanese, the Italians. Then they really scraped the bottom of the barrel when they forced old people to bear arms.

The Germans have caused so much misery to so many families in the world this last 70 years it is time they took a rest.'

TOM BARKER

DUAL PURPOSE FURNITURE: MORRISON SHELTER/PING-PONG TABLE

MEMORIES OF AN EVACUEE   LOCATION GLOUCESTERSHIRE

At the end of October 1940:

'After several weeks of sleepless nights and seeing the glow in the sky when they set the docks on fire, my family thought I should get out of London as I was expecting my first baby.

My mother had a cousin living in the village of Enstone, who with her husband managed the Litchfield Arms there (Mr and Mrs Peachey). They were full up and Phyllis Parsons (Johns wife) happened to be in the local shop, Adams Stores, when this was discussed and agreed to have me, so that is how I came to Fulwell.

I very soon adapted to country life, with having oil lamps and going down to the pump for water. David was five at the time and Tony was 13 or 14 (Phyllis's sons) and they worked hard in the garden – quite remarkable at that age and we never went short of vegetables.

THE MOST ENDURING OF WWII SLOGANS

I soon got to know the people of Fulwell; Mrs Gould, the Benfield family, Mrs Simons, Mrs Bull, Connie, Mrs Canning and Ruby. I think it was a Miss Haws who lived at the farmhouse and the top house in the village was occupied by the district nurse.

We were both leaving men's wives, Phyllis and I, so we had a lot in common. I can't remember when John went to France but I remember him telling me about Dunkirk. He never said much about it only that it had been a dreadful time.

Three weeks before my baby was due to be born I had to go into Oxford to Ruskin college with other London mothers to wait for the birth.

Angela was born on the 21st January and a fortnight later I brought her back to Fulwell. Phyllis was a great help to me having had children of her own, Angela flourished, she was a very good baby. I can remember John saying, on going back after a weeks leave 'I have been here a week and I haven't heard that baby cry!'

Angela was baptised in Spelsbury church on March 23rd 1941.

I so appreciated the countryside, the stalks of corn in the fields, Mr Canning with his team of horses. Life was very peaceful, Phyllis and I would walk to Enstone to meet David from school and do any shopping at Adams.

We often went into Chippy for the pictures, it was 9d return on the bus (that is about 3 pence now). We had the butcher from Charlbury call and a Mr Luker from Enstone with bread and cakes, also the Co-op from Chippy with groceries. We managed very well with our rations. I remember Mr Benfield killing a pig and we had back bone pudding which was delicious and we also had rabbit at times. We often saw Aunty Mary (John's sister) and little Pat and John, I still keep in touch with Aunty Mary. At Christmas 1941 my husband came on embarkation leave in November and he sailed for the Far East ending up in Burma, he was in the Royal Corps of Signals (The Forgotten Army). I never saw him again until after the war.

I will never forget Angela's first Christmas, she was taken ill and Dr O'Shea from Chippy had her admitted into Chippy Cottage Hospital where she spent a few days. I remember the kindness of Aunty Mary. She put me up so as to be near for visiting.

Every Sunday afternoon two priests used to come from the Mansion at Enstone to give the boys (David and Tony) instruction in the Catholic faith. I used to take Angela for a walk in her pram usually up the track to Ditchley. It was a picture in the springtime with wild flowers each side of the road.

YOUR COURAGE
YOUR CHEERFULNESS
YOUR RESOLUTION
WILL BRING
US VICTORY

RAISING MORALE
– A VITAL FACTOR
IN WARTIME

During the war there was a 'salute to the soldier' week at Ditchley.
Lady Astor was there and she gave a short talk. There were crowds
there, but she spotted Mrs Gould with her five children. She came
and spoke to her and she must have been impressed for she took
off her lovely white hat with cherries on, and said 'I take my hat off
to you'. I never saw Mrs Gould wearing it!

Although things looked very black at times I never once thought we
could lose the war. We always knew when Churchill was at Ditchley
for the weekend as we would see the Home Guard go by and the
Post Office vans. As the war progressed we saw changes, the Enstone
'Drome' was used for gliders and the American troops came and laid
large bombs all along the sides of the road ready for D-day. John

was wounded in North Africa and it was a very worrying time for Phyllis, he was eventually invalided out of the army. I spoke about going back to London but he would not hear of it 'I was only too thankful to have you here' he said and as the flying bombs were raining down on London I was glad to stay.

So the war ended and I returned home to begin my married life again. I have kept in touch all these years and remember all the kindness I received from the Parsons family with gratitude.'

MRS SHEARER

STOLEN FRUIT – A LONDON CHILDHOOD LOCATION LONDON

'It wasn't much fun being a small kid at that time. It was too scary. London was a smoggy city, filled with grey skies, grey fog, rainy days and one seldom saw a blue sky or sunshine. Or so it seemed. And indoors, it always seemed to be night. Everyone had black curtains on the windows so that no light would escape into the street and, more importantly, be seen from the German airplanes flying overhead. Lights could show them a good place to drop a bomb. Besides, electricity was expensive and not to be used if not necessary.

My dad was away in the army, somewhere in Europe and my mother was very nervous. She was a young woman in her mid 20's, with a little girl (me) and a new baby, and she wanted someone to look after her and there wasn't anyone to do it. So she cried a lot, and when the siren would go off to warn of an air-raid, she would scream in fear. I always felt responsible for her, like I should be her mother and take care of her. But I was only three and four and five and six and didn't know how, except by not being a burden.

In the beginning, the bombing was at night. She would tell me to quickly! quickly! put on a sweater or coat and shoes and run downstairs. I would hide under the kitchen table until she had dressed herself and wrapped up the baby. Then we would run through the long, narrow garden to the air-raid shelter. It seemed always to be night and dark, with sirens screaming and wailing.

The shelter was simply some corrugated steel sheets made into a shed against the brick garden wall, with a sloping roof. It had a dirt floor and two wooden benches inside on which to sit. No heat, no light. Mother brought candles if she remembered, or else we sat in the dark. If a stranger was on the street when the sirens began, they could knock at any house door and be taken in to the shelter, and spend the night there.

Mother was always complaining about the rations. She wasn't a good cook and didn't know how to make exotic things like puddings or any treats, so our food was very simple. Mostly something boiled or fried. There was often nothing – nothing at all – to eat and we got used to being hungry.

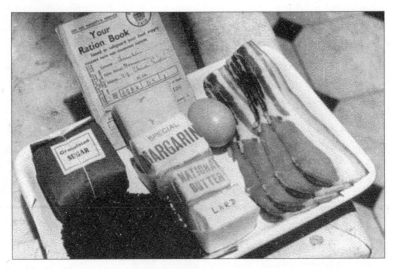

A WEEKS RATION ON A SINGLE PLATE

One afternoon I went down to the bottom of the garden and found some boxes so that I could climb onto the roof of the air-raid shelter. Then, from there I could climb onto the top of the brick wall between our garden and that of the old lady next door. She had a pear tree, loaded with fruit. With a long stick I was able to reach some of the branches and bring them over the wall. Then I picked off the pears and tossed them down into our garden. She saw from her window, and came out waving her walking stick at me, telling me to leave her pears alone! I quickly scooted down off the wall, down the roof of the shelter, onto the boxes and back to safety. Whew! A close escape – and five beautiful pears to eat! I ate three right away, and took two inside to give to mother.

Other thefts occurred. At the end of the garden was a gate to an alleyway. On the other side of the alleyway was a fence, and behind that fence the train ran by.

The stationmaster had a little hut there, and he planted strawberries in the ground between the railroad tracks and the fence. Strawberries! Beautiful, red, sweet strawberries, right there in the city! Amazing. So, with a bent stick, and lots of patience, I could slowly, slowly bring a vine close enough to the fence to put my fingers through the fencing and pick a strawberry. Oh, it was so delicious! Heavenly. But then the stationmaster would see me there and come out with his fist raised, shouting 'Leave my strawberries alone!', and I would escape to the safety of our garden.

The City Authorities would regularly send people (women with small children) out of the City, into the country for safety. During one of these exits from the city, we were staying with a woman and her four daughters in a big farm house. These pretty girls were being dated by American soldiers and one day one of the soldiers brought an extraordinary treat to the house. It was something I had never seen before and that the girls had not seen in four or five years – a fresh orange! The orange was peeled, with everyone standing around the table watching. Then, it was carefully divided into segments, and each person got one segment. First we licked it, so no drop of juice could escape. Then, we took tiny nibbles, letting the juice come slowly into our mouths, and held it there. Don't swallow too fast! Then take another tiny nibble, until finally, the whole slice was gone. How terrible that there was no more. Seeing what a great success the gift had been, the soldier decided he had to be a hero to the nth degree.

A few days later he came back with his friend and a carton, a whole carton of cans of sliced peaches. Twelve cans. Twelve CANS! Wow! What to do with such booty? Urgent conversations took place. Suggestions made and discarded. Finally, with everyone watching, the carton, less one can, was taken down into the cellar and buried under the heap of coal. Then, everyone was sworn to secrecy. No one must tell what was hidden there.

Sometime passed, and one day there was a knock at the door. Military police. They wanted to search the house for stolen contraband from the PX. My heart was racing… would we go to jail? Would the soldiers be arrested? What would happen? They searched everywhere, but did not want to get dirty moving the heap of black, sooty coal, and so the peaches were undiscovered. But we all felt horribly guilty whenever a can was opened, and it spoiled the pleasure in eating those sweet slices.'

PAMELA

MEMORIES OF KENNITH

Here is a moving story that shows the destructive nature of war on a very personal level:

'It was 1943, quite near the end of the war. I was in my house when the sirens went off. My family dashed to the stairs and sat under them as we awaited the sounds and screams as the bomb hit the port. We knew it was aimed at the port next to where we lived as all the other ports had been bombed. As the plane came nearer, my whole body became tense. I felt as if something was going to go wrong, like the bomb would miss the port and hit us instead. I was right. The bomb missed the port and hit our house. Luckily, the bomb hit the other side of the house which gave us all time to get out. Everyone survived, apart from my brother, Kennith. He got hit on his way home after playing outside with his friends. He was rushing home when the siren went off. Kennith was the youngest child out of the four children my mother had. She tried so hard to keep the family together after Kennith died. I miss him terribly.'

RACHEL BOULTON

LUCKY AT LUNCH

'When war broke out we lived in Catford. I was attending the school there when it was bombed and so many children and teachers were killed. It happened at lunch time and I had gone home for lunch, which I rarely did, so I am lucky to be here to tell my story. I am a long way from home now, living a very different life in California, but memories of those war years are as fresh to me now as if it happened last year.'

HAZEL MATHESON

FRIENDLY FIREWORKS LOCATION LONDON

'My parents had a laundry business in London during the war and one of their customers was our MP [Beverly Baxter I believe, but am not sure]. He arranged for our family to obtain passes to the House of Commons for the VE Day celebrations. It must have been on the evening of May 8th 1945, shortly before my 15th birthday that we were seated in an open-air roof garden in very balmy weather at the Parliament buildings. From there we watched thousands of people celebrating in the streets below, but most impressive were the fireworks. One of the bridges, which I think was probably London Bridge, had effigies of the King and Queen, the Union Jack and Royal Crest in fireworks and I believe Sir Winston Churchill too, and these seemed to burn for a considerable period of time. This, combined with the fireworks bursting in the air was such an impressive sight that it remains quite vivid in my mind, I don't think I have ever seen such a fireworks display since. As the evening wore on, Mr Churchill came out into the garden to shake hands with as many people as he could and we were of course delighted to shake his hand. Although he had obviously imbibed well, as he puffed away on the ubiquitous cigar he was very coherent and easy to talk to.'

JIM WILCOX

SHADES OF WAR ·LOCATION OXFORDSHIRE

This refers to a time five short years after the ending of WW2, as you will see as in most of history there is no distinct line where the privations of conflict cease:

'I arrived at RAF Brize Norton in August 1950. Our Barracks still had holes in the ceiling and Spitfires, Hurricanes, Meteors and Gliders in storage. There was still a strong presence of the Second World War. Rationing was still in effect, and the bombed out buildings in London left a lasting impression on me. So much that I spent almost 40 years there and married two of your lovely ladies.'

JOHN HATFIELD (USA)

WAR CHANGES EVERYTHING LOCATION KENT AND LONDON

'When the war started there were a lot of changes about what we could and couldn't do. Until the start of the war, children used to play in the streets until it was dark, we had all sorts of street games we would play but with the threat of air-raids we could no longer do this. A play centre was opened up near our school, we used to go there after school, we had Brownies, Girl Guides, Boy Scouts and Cubs. We also used to take part in different activities, as we got older, we were allowed to join in the dance that was held once a week, most of us could do a waltz or quick-step.

At home we used to play board games, listen to the wireless while knitting or sewing, there wasn't much wool about, but my mum and nan used to buy second-hand jumpers from the market and unpick them, the wool would then be rounded into skeins and washed. My dad was always trying to help me with my school work, we didn't have home-work, but he used to let me fill in his time-sheets for him, I always had to do my best hand-writing, he was so proud of this. We spent a lot of time reading, I used to love animal stories, one of my favourites was Rudyard Kipling's Jungle Book, another was Black Beauty, there was also a regular story in one of my comics about Black Bob, a lovely sheep dog, I used to love to draw the animals. My nan was given an old fashion book, it had sketches of fashion, I used to copy these and even started to design my own dresses. Dad used to bring home lots of used bus tickets, he would get these from the box on the bus, I would spend hours making up little models and all sorts of furniture. Another thing I loved playing with was Plasticine. I made lots of models with this.

MOST HAD NO
ALTERNATIVE BUT TO
MAKE-DO AND MEND

EYES WERE ALWAYS ON THE SKIES

People often talk about the hardship that rationing bought, but I suppose because we were so poor before the war, it didn't seem any different to us. The job that my dad got just before the war started was with a builder, he learned to do scaffolding, and at that time there was a great demand for this sort of work. Because my mum now had regular house-keeping money we could have all sorts of things that we were unable to have before. We had lots of stews with dumplings, mum used neck of lamb to make the stews because this was a cheap meat, you got more for your ration, the meat was rationed by price rather that weight, you could have rump steaks if you wanted, but because it was so expensive you only got a tiny piece. Liver, hearts, brains, rabbit, sheep's head, pigs' trotters and pigs' heads were all sold in what was called the offal shop. There was also whale meat but this wasn't very popular. This shop was opened twice a week and people would start to queue outside about 6.30 in the morning, the shop didn't open until nine so there was quite a long queue by the time it opened. Fish was also used a lot, we used to have herrings, eels and conger eel. The fish and chip shop was also very popular, it was so cheap compared to today's prices even allowing for inflation. One thing you had to do was take your own newspaper to wrap it in, you were given a small piece of white paper just to line the newspaper, but if you didn't have your newspaper you couldn't have any fish and chips. I have never been able to get over how expensive it is to go into a fish and chip shop these days.

A VI IN FLIGHT – HITLER'S LATE SURPRISE

The baker shop near us used to sell yesterday's bread and cakes cheap. You could buy a really big bag of yesterday's cakes for a penny, also two large loaves of yesterday's bread for a penny. Mum often used to make bread pudding, currants were scarce but she used to cut up apples and carrots, sugar was also rationed, but with plenty of mixed spice it tasted just as good.

I mentioned earlier that we used to dance at our playcentre, one dance that I really loved was the jitterbug. My dad learned this from the American soldiers who were billeted at a hotel near us. They used to go in the pub that my dad used and jitterbug with any lady or girl who would give them a chance, they taught my dad to jitterbug and he taught me. This later became the Rock and Roll, something I still do to this day. At Christmas, the American soldiers used to give all the local children a party, everyone was given a present from America, it came in the form of a parcel full of goodies, one thing I always remember was the lovely scented soap. My mum always used Fairy soap, I don't think you needed so many coupons for that. The parties were held in the hotel where the soldiers were billeted, there was a really big Christmas tree with lights and a fairy at the top, I had never seen one like this before. I remember one Christmas one of the soldiers played the piano and sang *'Jeanie with the Light Brown Hair'*. I still hear that song from time to time and it brings back lovely memories. Christmas was always pretty wonderful, we never seemed to go short. Because my mum came from such a big family, everyone used to club together and spend Christmas at my nan and granddad's house. Their house was an old tenement house with two rooms on each of the three floors, it was next door to a stable, my granddad used to work there. Anyway, back to Christmas. All the children used to sleep in one room, there were about a dozen of us and all the mums and dads slept in another room. Everyone brought something for the Christmas dinner, the main dinner being a capon (a very large chicken specially bred for Christmas) that the stable owner used to give us, this was granddad's Christmas box. Christmas pudding was a wonderful invention of my nan's, everything would go into it and it would be boiled in the laundry copper for hours. Somehow all the children seemed to have lovely presents, one year I had a lovely baby doll with a real china head, another year I had a three wheel bicycle. Another present I always loved was a children's sewing machine, it could sew real stitches, I used to make dolls dresses on it.

At the start of the war, I lived with my mum and dad in a small terraced house, it had two rooms upstairs and two rooms down stairs, there was a bedroom and a living room. Everything was done in the living room as there was no kitchen. The toilet was in the back yard. I lived with mum and dad downstairs and another family lived in the two rooms upstairs. We were lucky, there was only three of us, the family upstairs had three children. My mum had her name down on the council list and early in 1940 we were allocated a council flat. It was a one bedroom flat but had a little scullery, but the toilet was still outside on the landing. Although we didn't have to share with anyone, it was on the top floor, there were six stories, so we had quite a climb to get to it. Early in 1941 when my mum was expecting my brother, the council gave us a flat on the first floor because my mum was unable to climb the stairs. It still only had one bedroom but as this flat had an inside toilet we felt in the lap of luxury. All this time I haven't mentioned bathrooms, because we never had one. Once a week we used to borrow my nan's tin bath, it was put in front of the fire. Mum used to put the clothes horse round it with towels draped on it to give us a bit of privacy, the water was heated on the gas cooker in large pots, this took ages and even when we were in the bath more pots were put on the stove to keep the bath water warm. Until my brother was born in July 1941 I was bathed first, then my mum would get in and have a bath and then my dad would get in last, we could only do this once a week because it used to use up so much gas to heat the water and the gas was expensive. We used to top and tail in the kitchen sink the rest of the week. Of course when my brother came along I had to take second place in the bath, but I didn't mind.

No one had anywhere to do their washing so everyone went to my nan's house, nan had a backyard with a big sink, a mangle and a gas copper. I remember once helping my nan with the washing – I was standing on a chair besides the sink and fell in, I was soaked. My nan didn't have anything to put on me so she put one of my grand-dads jumpers on me. I used to stand on a chair beside the mangle and help nan to turn the handle, the hardest thing to do was getting the washing dry. Sometimes it would take all week to dry and then we would start all over again.

A LAND GIRL
GETTING STUCK IN

My granddad had a cellar to the house so he turned it into an air-raid shelter for him and nan. My mum and dad would take me and my brother down to the London Underground at Euston Station. I used to love to go down there, I made a few friends and we used to ride back and forward on the trains, I don't think we were supposed to do this, but no one ever said anything to us. My dad would go back upstairs to join his pals on fire-watch duty and we would stay down and sleep on bunks until the morning, very often when we came up the skies were a bright red where the bombs had been dropped, As we lived at Euston, we were right in the middle of it all.

I was twelve years old when the war ended, all the mums and dads arranged a really big street party. We built a big bonfire. The wood for the fire came from a factory that had been bombed out, although it was damaged, there wasn't much left of it by the time the wood was taken for the bonfire. That year was the first time we were allowed to make a guy for Guy Fawkes, I dressed up as Hitler and I dressed my brother up like Carmen Miranda (she was a Mexican singer). It was also the first time that we had been able to get fireworks. There were sparklers, bangers, rockets and Catherine Wheels, we really thought they were wonderful, but when I see the sort of fireworks that are about today, they were tiny in comparison. I think that one of the best things that happened for me was that my mum was able to take me to the cinema more. She had always been afraid to take me while the war was on, so that became a really big treat. We were also allowed out more, so we spent a lot more time at the park. Also I used to go swimming a lot.

I hadn't realised what a terrible thing the war had been until the end. It wasn't until I read in the newspapers about all the terrible things that had been done to people in the concentration camps. It wasn't until it was all over that I realised what a narrow escape we had all had.'

PATRICIA TOS

THE DISASTER OF FRECKLETON   LOCATION NORTHWEST

In war there are always innocent casualties. Sometimes, for purposes of maintaining morale during WW2 some tragedies were not widely reported. Of such incidents there were many. Here is an account of just one.

'It was August 23rd, 1944. The weather that day was awful. There had been lots of heavy rain, thunder and noise. The wind so rough that trees had been torn down. It was one of the worst storms I have ever seen. I was walking along the road when I heard this terrible noise of engines roaring and roaring. Then I saw this dark shape slide out of the rain. It just fell out of the air and hit the Sad Sack Café on the north side of the road and then just careered over to the other side and hit the school. I was just stunned by the sight. I could not believe what I was seeing. The noise was so awful I have nightmares about it even today, all these years after. I was so scared I just ran home to tell my family, but I met them on the way as they had heard the crash. It was such a terrible sight. It looked as if the whole street was on fire. We could not see the school for the flames. I can see it today as clearly as I did then. My mum was not a fool and realised there was nothing she could do. There was a smell of burning and fuel in the air and smoke everywhere. We stayed for a few minutes and waited for someone to come and start to do something, then we went home. It was not until later that we heard what had happened. It was the most terrible day I can remember. Just about everyone we knew had lost someone when that plane crashed. It was months before some of the older children, who survived because they were not in the part of the building hit, were able to go back to school.'

Here is a relatively brief account of what happened:

At 10.30am, August 23rd, 1944, one of the B-24 H-20 42-50291 Liberator aircraft – named 'Classy Chassis II', that had just been repaired at the nearby American Air Force base at Warton – was being flight tested. The pilot was 1st Lieutenant John Bloemendal. After a normal take-off from runway 08 the B-24 headed out over the Lancashire countryside, accompanied by a second B-24, 42-1353 being test flown by 1st Lieutenant Pete Manassero. Over the radio, Bloemendal called Manassero's attention to the cloud formation towards the south-southeast. It was a very impressive sight and looked like a 'thunderhead' according to Manassero.

In less than five minutes after the B-24 left Warton a telephone call reached the base from BAD 1 (Burtonwood), warning of a violent storm approaching the Preston area and immediately an order was issued recalling both Bloemendal's aircraft and that being flown by 1st Lieutenant Pete Manassero.

By the time the two B-24's arrived back over Warton, the storm was at its height. Witnesses relate the rain was so heavy that it was impossible to see across the road. The storm assumed proportions of an almost supernatural quality; thunder and lightning rolled across the sky and the wind was of such ferocity as to uproot trees and smash hen huts on a nearby farm. The sky turned an ominous black, and the whole district was plunged into darkness, even though it was a summer day, making it impossible to see indoors without the aid of artificial light. A contemporary local newspaper reported a trail of destruction across the northwest. Hutton Meteorological Station, which was fairly clear of the storm on the other side of the river, recorded wind velocity of nearly 60mph, with water spouts being observed in the Ribble estuary and flash flooding in Southport and Blackpool. Although the official report states that no further radio contact was made by Bloemendal with Control, radio conversations monitored by Warton's tower indicated that the two B-24 pilots had abandoned their attempts to land and were heading north to hold clear until the storm abated. This is what happened next in Pete Manassero's own words:

'As we drew near the field, I drew further out to be in position to land (as) number two. We let down to 500 feet and about four miles northwest of the field we encountered rain and it became heavier with less visibility as we neared the approach to Runway 08. On the base leg position Lt Bloemendal let down his gear (sic) and I did the same. Shortly after this I lost sight of Bloemendal's aircraft. As I flew over Lytham, I started a left turn to start the approach. At this time I heard Lt Bloemendal notify 'Faram' that he was pulling up the wheels and going around (this transmission recorded at Control as being between the two aircraft). I was then over the Wash (sic) and could not see the ground and had to fly on instruments. I then called Lt Bloemendal and told him we had better head north and get out of the storm. He answered 'OK'. I then told him I would take a heading of about 330 degrees. He said 'Roger'. That was the last I heard from Lt. Bloemendal. I flew about four or five minutes on a heading of about 330 degrees before breaking out of the storm. I then called Lt Bloemendal and asked if he was OK, and did not get a reply.'

The official report into the crash summarised that the exact cause was unknown, though it was the opinion of the investigating committee that the pilot made an error in his judgement of the violence of the storm. They concluded that Lt. Bloemendal had not fully realised the danger until he made his approach to land, by which time he had insufficient altitude and speed to manoeuvre, given the violent winds and downdrafts he must have encountered during his attempt to withdraw from the area. It was also thought possible that structural failure may have occurred in the extreme conditions, though it was noted that the aircraft was so completely destroyed as to make any such investigation impossible. Finally, it was recommended that pilots trained in the United States and then being sent to England, should be emphatically warned about the dangers of British thunderstorms. It was noted that many such pilots believed that British storms were little more than showers compared to those encountered in the southern United States and saw no danger in them, whereas they could be every bit as dangerous, though much less frequent.

The two aircraft had been caught in the worst storm ever recorded in that part of Britain. The plane crashed into the Holy Trinity Church School in Freckleton. Eyewitnesses reported that as fast as the storm had started it stopped. 38 five-year-old children and two teachers perished in the fire, as well as the three-man crew of the B-24 and some people who were sheltering from the storm, across Lytham Road in the Sad Sack Café. Thirty-six of the children, and their teachers, were laid to rest together in the churchyard cemetery. Only three five-year-old children survived and they spent about two years in and out of hospitals. One was a boy named George Madden whose home had been in the south of London. The others were George Carey and Ruby Whittle.

Among the casualties in the Sad Sack Café were six RAF men: four of them were killed and two injured. All were members of 22 Aircrew Handling Unit (22 AHU), a holding unit for aircrew at RAF Kirkham.

The Freckleton disaster is regarded as one of the worst disasters on British soil of WWII.

As far as I have been able to ascertain the story did not receive as much Press attention as it deserved; probably because on the same day Paris had been liberated.

JOHN, FORMERLY OF FRECKLETON

WAR IS DECLARED   LOCATION WARWICKSHIRE

This is an extract from the story of Peter Porter:

'The day before war broke out we were all told to put our uniforms on and fly the aircraft to various places in England to disperse them. I was detailed to go to Castle Bromwich with a Tiger Moth. On arrival there I looked up and to my astonishment I saw a barrage balloon appear out of the cloud at about 700-800 feet. I found out afterwards that there were four balloons at that height around the aerodrome. We had had no prior notification of this. However, fortunately, there were no accidents so it all passed off without any comment. Two of us went along to the police station to tell the sergeant in charge that we wanted to be billeted, and he came along with us while we chose where we would like to be housed. We drove around a bit until we finally found a nice big double fronted house and went to see if the lady would let us billet there. She said she didn't know to start with and would have to ask her husband. It turns out that he was a butcher with two or three shops, and when he showed up he said that he would be only too pleased to have us and that we could bring our wives up as well. And so we went down and picked them up and had a very pleasant fortnight with this Mr Darrel, who became a very sincere friend. It wasn't long before the other instructor and myself were moved over to Elmdon, which was the main aerodrome for Birmingham. Although today it has now been upgraded and expanded to become Birmingham International Airport, Elmdon at this time was only a grass airfield with no runways. Once over at Elmdon, my wife and I went to stay with one of her cousins who had a house near Solihul. Her husband owned a tyre factory just outside of Birmingham so we had no trouble getting tyres for our cars, even in those days of severe shortages. We stayed there for some months when eventually Doris became pregnant. We then thought that it would be a good thing if we could get into a furnished house of our own and managed to find one not very far away. We moved in there until my wife became too large and she decided that she would like to go home to her mother in Chelmsford, Essex. So I bundled her off to her mother's and I moved into digs with another instructor by the name of Tom Walls. His father was an actor and had played the lead part in a film called 'Rookery Nook' along with many others. One day while we were grounded at Elmdon, because of low cloud, another instructor and myself had been down to the local pub for a glass of beer when we heard an aircraft in the area followed by some big thumps. We assumed that there was something going on at the aerodrome and immediately got in the car and drove straight back there. Once we arrived, we met the CO at the top of the airport building, dressed only in his pyjamas, with a pistol in his hand waiting for the aircraft to come back. In the meantime it had dropped four or five bombs on the aerodrome, before scattering back into the cloud again and vanishing. However, the bombs that had been dropped left big craters in the grass airfield, including one that was only twenty yards away from the main building – definitely a close call! In the meantime the baby was on the way and Doris was taken up to Danbury Palace in Essex. Danbury Palace was a property belonging to a General and his wife that had been turned into a maternity home for the duration of the war. My son, Peter, was born on September 21st, 1940, during a German air raid on the area. That turned out to be quite a night and, after taking care of Doris, the doctor actually had to help extinguish some fire bombs on the way to give her mother the good news that all was well. Peter was named after Flying Officer Peter Scott, who was my co-pilot during my training at Montrose, and was also the Best Man at my wedding. I was then given a very welcome week of compassionate leave to go home and see my son and my wife.'

PETER PORTER, ROYAL AIR FORCE

TEMPERED FOR PEACE   LOCATION SOMEWHERE IN ENGLAND

'The thing about living through that period was that it gave you a greater strength to handle life in general. Being brought up amongst all that devastation things could only get better. Which of course in real terms they have.'

TONY GOWEN

Part three
RECIPES FROM THE HOME FRONT

YOUR EVACUEES!

Extra mouths to feed

To make the most and get the best

out of every scrap of meat

use

BISTO

'Potato Pete'

Part three
RECIPES FROM THE HOME FRONT

Betty Armitage lived in Norfolk during WW2 and kept a diary from the first day of the conflict to the last. She also wrote down her favourite recipes and, alongside most, some idea of the kind of life she led and the people she cooked for and looked after.

Here is a selection of some of her culinary delights.

BEEF LOAF

'There is nothing like having something to carve for a meal. This loaf, although simple and quick, is very popular. There were some young men from Swanton Morley who came to see me in 1940 that liked a good tuck in and that day I was just about out of anything to give them. I made this loaf and what with some vegetables I fed them until they nearly burst.'

INGREDIENTS

1 tin of corned beef

1 egg

3oz of dry breadcrumbs

1oz margarine

2 onions chopped, keep half an onion to slice for top

1 sliced carrot

1 bay leaf

Salt and pepper

Cut corned beef into very small pieces and mix with breadcrumbs and onion. Grease a baking tin of suitable size to take mixture. Melt margarine and mix into mixture well, season as you will. Beat egg as well as you can and stir into mixture as a binder. Put mixture into prepared tin and press down well with a level top. Arrange sliced carrot and onion on the top. Bake in moderate oven for three quarters of an hour. Take care to sprinkle some water on it from time to time to stop top from drying out too much.

Serve with vegetables in season.

AUNT CATHERINE'S SHEPHERD'S PIE

'Late summer, 1943, Jack and I helped George out behind the bar during a darts match when Beryl was visiting her mother. Some American airmen, who had only recently arrived in this country, came in and were made welcome. I remember the relief we all felt when they entered the war. I often wonder how they must have felt coming all this way to fight in what for them is a foreign war. Like most of the other fliers they were all quite young and as I write this in 1944, I know how much they have all sacrificed. Some of the young men I met that day are no longer with us. During that evening in 1943 they tucked in to some pasties I had made for the occasion and remarked how much they missed home cooking. I asked them if they would like to come round for a meal as they would always be welcome and John 'S' said it was very 'gracious and kind' of me to offer. He was a very polite boy. Some two or three weeks later he came with four of his mates one Sunday and I cooked what Jack says he can eat at anytime, my Aunt Catherine's Shepherds Pie, with beef they kindly brought with them.

As we sat down to eat, one of them said 'five flying eights sit down to eat'*. We didn't know then what a heavy price they would pay for their courage.'

INGREDIENTS

2lbs of minced beef

2 good sized onions

Thyme

1/4lb tomatoes

2 good sprigs of parsley

8 large boiled potatoes

1 egg

Cup of milk

1/4oz butter or margarine

Heat large deep frying pan to good heat. Fry beef briskly until well browned stirring all the time. It is important that the meat is really browned with little sign of grey. Remove from heat. Add chopped onion and return to a lower heat until onion is just starting to appear clear. Add stock, a little thyme, Oxo, salt and pepper. Stir thoroughly and cook at a simmer for five to ten minutes. Put mixture in large casserole. Drain potatoes, mash well stirring in milk as you go, butter or margarine and egg until smooth and stiff. Form egg shapes of

---

* possibly a reference to the '44th Bomb Group Flying Eightballs'

potato mixture by pushing into the bowl of a large table spoon. Arrange potato eggs to cover meat mixture in casserole. Cook in a hot oven for about 20 to 25 minutes or until surface of potatoes is brown and crisp. The most important part of this recipe is the browning of the beef. This must be done properly until the meat is really browned or the flavour will not be right.

Serve with carrots, peas and mild beer. Serves six.

CHRISTMAS PIE

'Some things remind you of times and you cannot help it. Fresh mown grass reminds of spring days, eating sandwiches with some of the boys and girls I have toured with over so many years. Hot days, lying on our backs looking up at the birds wheeling around a clear blue sky. In hot weather it was always funny how people used to behave, not giving a care for how they looked as long as they got the sun on them. When I smell my mincemeat pie cooking I am back in Mrs Chappell's lodgings in 1915. We had had a bad year that year, what with the war and all, but her Charlie was home on leave unexpected and we had a right old knees up. Ellen, one of the chorus, took a real shine to Charlie. If his mother had known what went on that Christmas I don't know what she would have done.'

INGREDIENTS

12oz shortcrust pastry

2 large cooking apples

1/2lb mincemeat

1 large tablespoon of sugar

Roll half the pastry and line pie tin. Finely chop apples, mix with sugar and mincemeat. Spread over lined pie tin. Cover with remaining pastry. Bake for 40 minutes in hot oven. Serve piping-hot with cream or brandy butter. Can be eaten cold.

DUMPLINGS

'Where would we be without dumplings. Nothing fills like a good old dumpling. And they are so easy to make. I try to make them every-time I cook a stew because they are so filling and good for you. On a cold day they are one of the life saving foods I think.'

INGREDIENTS

1/2lb of flour

Salt and pepper

3oz margarine

Water

Mix flour, salt and pepper in a bowl. Rub margarine in well. Add cold water a little at a time and mix to a stiff dough. Roll into balls of same size. The easiest way to cook them is to place them on top of stew for the last hour of cooking. Easy and one of the best foods in the world.

I make a good Soup! *Says* 'POTATO PETE'

'POTATO PETE' HIGHLIGHTS THE MERITS OF THE GOOD OLD POTATO

EGGS ON STRAW POTATOES

'This recipe was given to me by Elsie Skipper when she popped in to borrow my *People's Friends* for her sister who was laid up with a bad leg months and months ago.

It is very simple and the boys from Coltishall really enjoy it for supper or at any time really. Bob 'J' liked them so much he gave me one of his poems by way of a thank you the first time I cooked it for him. Better than fish and chips he said. I shall always remember his poem, it isn't very long':

RED SKY
I ride a beast with a fiery breath,
It paws the wind,
It spits forth death.

For two servings, grate two large potatoes coarsely. Mix in a little salt and pepper to taste. Pat into rounds about 4 to 5 inches across and no more than an inch thick. Put fat into frying pan and raise to a good heat. Fry briskly at first and then turn down the heat. Cook until golden brown on the underside so that it forms a crisp crust to enable them to be turned over without breaking up. The natural juices help make a tasty crust. Fry until brown on both sides, do not leave to burn. Fry eggs and serve on top of potato cakes. It is best to have two frying pans on the go so the potato cakes do not cool waiting for the eggs. This is a very healthy meal to start the day with and a fine way to taste the potatoes at their best.

GRIDDLE CAKES

'I cooked these on the first day I ever worked. I must have made thousands and thousands of them. The woman who showed me how to make them, Mrs Todd, she was from Gateshead, said it was the simplest of all recipes and one that would always be useful. She was right too as these cakes have fed many when money has been tight. Margarine is not as good as butter but will do.'

INGREDIENTS

1lb flour

Milk

5oz butter or margarine

Teaspoon of salt

Mix everything together adding milk as you go. Make it into a nice stiff dough, this must not be sticky so be careful not to add too much milk. Roll out to quarter inch thick and cook on a hot griddle.

Serve buttered on their own or with jam. Makes a nice simple tea.

CARROTS ON STICKS MAKE A DELICIOUS TREAT!

MACARONI AND TOMATO

'Macaroni is a good nourishing and cheap food. These days it is important to keep ourselves fit and active and well fed. I use fresh tomatoes when in season or tinned when they are not. They both work just as well. When we had a traveller staying at the pub once he was surprised as he only had ever had macaroni in a milk pudding before. He was very pleased and ordered seconds. This recipe uses rather a lot of cheese so it is really a special dish and has to be saved for.'

INGREDIENTS

1/2lb of macaroni

1/2lb of tomatoes tinned or fresh

4oz cheese

1 onion

2oz margarine

parsley

salt and pepper

tablespoon or two of breadcrumbs

Cook macaroni until just soft in usual way. Melt margarine in a saucepan then add chopped onion and cook until soft. Then add tomatoes, parsley, salt and pepper to taste. Leave on low heat for twenty five minutes keeping an eye on it. Add macaroni and grated cheese and stir into sauce gently. Turn out into a well greased oven dish, cover with breadcrumbs. Bake in hot oven for fifteen minutes.

Serve with vegetables or bread.

MAGGIE WALSHE'S BACON PIE

'Maggie Walshe was one of my best friends. We used to do every-thing together. We lost track of each other in 1914 and I often wonder where she is and what she is doing. This was one of her favourite recipes and many is the time we shared a bottle of stout and one of these.'

INGREDIENTS

Shortcrust pastry

4 rashers of good bacon with not too much fat

2 eggs

Chopped sage

1 onion chopped

Mashed potato

Milk

Butter or margarine

Salt and pepper

Line the pie dish with pastry. Lay two rashers of the bacon in the bottom and add just a little sage and onion. Season the mashed potato well and mix with butter or margarine and some milk, then cover bacon with the mixture. Pour over the beaten and seasoned eggs. Lay on the other two rashers of bacon. Cook in moderate oven for half an hour.

In good times use more bacon. It is a hearty pie and packs up well.

Serve with vegetables or on its own as a packed up meal.

MAGIC TREACLE TART

'When people go to a theatre I don't think they can understand how hard it is for all the boys and girls and how much they have to go through to make it all look so easy. I have seen some of the people I worked with crying with pain and the cold sometimes just before they are due to go on but as soon as they are on stage they do what they are paid to do. Not many of them were very well paid but they all gave the best performance they could. I used to like to give them a little treat if they were a bit miserable. My good old treacle tart usually did the trick. 'Magic' someone called it once so I do now. It is not always easy to get the stuff these days. It can be made without the lemon rind and juice, a little marmalade will do. When the war is over I will make it every week.'

INGREDIENTS

About three quarters of a pound of golden syrup

3 heaped tablespoons breadcrumbs (fresh not stale)

2 tablespoons of ground up almonds

Grated lemon rind

Lemon juice

2 or 3 tablespoons of cream

1 egg

Make enough pastry to cover a good sized pie plate. After covering pie plate add all the other ingredients mixed well. Bake in hot oven until golden. Keep an eye on it, let your eyes and nose tell you when it is done.

Serve whenever it is needed.

NIGHTFIGHTER STEW

'We had a competition among ourselves, Mavis, Beryl, Doris and me, to make the best meal we could with as little meat. This was my recipe. As we are being told to eat so many carrots for our eyesight I thought this would be tasty. If you take the trouble to see how to cook this it is very easy. The most difficult part is to get the cooking time right. Let your nose tell you.'

4lbs carrots

1lb potatoes

1/4 cup of flour

Oxo

Good sized onion

Worcester sauce

Water

Seasoning

Slice carrots and boil for ten minutes. Prepare a good sized oven dish. Slice cooked potatoes into neat slices. Add layer of carrots to dish, then a layer of sliced onion, then a layer of potato. Do this till you run out of potato, the rest is just carrot. Mix flour with half pint of water and Oxo – if you have enough use two cubes – seasoning and pour over top of mixture with a dash of Worcester sauce, and then pour in enough water to come halfway up the dish.

Cook in a moderate oven for an hour and a half. Best to keep an eye on it to see it has enough water.

Serve piping hot with dumplings or bread.

ONION SOUP
(Home Guard Soup)

Serves 4 (multiply quantity as necessary for more)

'This soup has been a favourite in my family since my great, great grandmother's day. I know this because I have the recipe in her own hand. Only people who do not like onions, and I don't know many of them, don't like it. I try to have some ready to eat all through the winter as it is one of the most warming and strengthening soups there is. I cook this for the Home Guard when they are on duty and it is cold. I just leave a big pan of it on the stove in the hall and they help themselves. Jack says that it tastes better when served with hot strong tea on a frosty night. His platoon call it 'Home Guard Soup'.'

INGREDIENTS

1 1/2lb of onions

1 1/2 pints of stock

1 teaspoon of flour

2oz butter or margarine

Pepper and salt

Place butter in thick bottomed pan and heat until it is bubbling. Slice or chop onions finely, add to pan and sprinkle with flour. Fry well moving about the pan all the time with a wooden spoon until they are about to turn brown. Pour on hot stock a little at a time stirring all the while. Add salt if required, and pepper for certain. When all stock is in pan bring to the boil and simmer gently for twenty-five minutes, when it is ready to serve. If necessary this soup may be kept hot on a stove for hours provided it is in a covered container. Serve with thick fresh bread and hot strong tea.

BETTY'S SATURDAY SCONES

'I must have made thousands of these in my time. When I worked in the tea shop in Coventry I used to make these every afternoon. We used to serve them hot with butter and home-made jam. Doris sells most on Fridays and Saturdays so when she places her order with me she just calls them 'Saturdays', and that's what her customers ask for when they buy from her. They have to be eaten very fresh and preferably when warm. Jennifer says that sitting in the garden of an afternoon in the sun with a plate of these and a bottle of Gordon's is her idea of heaven.

When I pack up food for anyone I try to put at least 4 of these in. When 'the boys' are off on leave and have a long journey I will try to put in half a dozen to keep them going.'

INGREDIENTS

3 cups plain flour

1/2 cupful dried fruit (raisins, sultanas)

1/2 cup approx. of milk, fresh or sour

1/4lb cooking fat

2 level dessert spoons of baking powder

1/2 cupful of sugar

Make up as you would ordinary short crust pastry, adding a little extra water or milk if after mixing well some dry material remains. Roll out dough, sprinkle on fruit, fold in half and roll again to 1/2 an inch thick then cut two-inch round shapes. Grease well a heavy frying pan and raise to a low heat. Place scones in pan and cook for about five minutes until risen. Turn over and cook in same way. These times are approximate. Cook for longer if not good colour or less if too brown. This is a simple recipe but needs patience to get right and you must watch them all the time they are cooking. But it is worth taking trouble over. They can be made without the dried fruit.

When I am cooking these for the shop I sometimes have three pans on the go at the same time.

SAUSAGES TUCKED UP IN BED

'Jack's favourite. He likes this everytime he comes for supper. It is a good thing most of the others like it too. His dad is a farmer in the Yorkshire Dales and only likes to have mutton or, in the spring, lamb on the table. He does not like to buy from the butcher. He sounds a close man with his money. Jack says his dad hopes he'll be back in time for lambing. Him and his friend Mick were very drunk last Tuesday and were put on a charge. They are only young and Mick is a rear-gunner, he told me he needs a drink to get by.'

A very good meal for 4-6 or more, especially if they are hard workers.

INGREDIENTS

1lb sausages

2 1/2lb mashed potatoes

1 pint of milk

1/4 pint of ale

1/4lb soaked dried peas

1/2 tablespoon each of parsley and sage.

2oz of margarine

Brush a dish for the oven with margarine. After boiling sausages, skin and quarter then lay in the dish. Boil peas, drain and add to dish. Dust lightly with pepper and salt. Pour in beer. Heat potatoes. Add margarine, pepper and salt, and milk after heating it, then beat mixture until smooth.

Spread mixture over sausages, smooth and brush with milk. Bake in hot oven for half an hour.

Serve with thick onion soup, fresh bread and stout.

SAMUEL JOHNSON'S STEAK AND KIDNEY PUDDING

'When I was working at the Aldwych Sir Hugo told me that at his club in London steak and kidney pudding had been the favourite dish since the days of old Sam Johnson, and the recipe I use was given by the cook from Sir Hugo's club. Can't do better than that, can you? I think Dr. Johnson would forgive me using an Oxo, after all there is a war on'.

1lb steak and kidney

Flour and suet (substitute hard vegetable fat)

1 medium onion

Flour for thickening

1/4 pint concentrated beef stock or 1/4 pint of water and 1 Oxo

Salt and pepper for seasoning

Line a large pudding basin with the pastry, keeping enough back for the top. Toss steak and kidney well in seasoned flour. Chop onion finely and crush well to release all the juices, this is the secret to a better flavour. Mix onion, meat and beef stock or crumbled Oxo. Put in pastry lined basin. Cover with water and add seasoned flour. Make top with remaining pastry and press into place, pressing edges well together. It is worth taking some time to make sure this job is done really well to keep all the flavour in. Cover with floured cloth and tie with string. Half fill saucepan with water and bring to boil. Place pudding in saucepan and boil gently for two hours, topping up saucepan if necessary. Serve with potatoes, carrots and peas.

TOAD IN THE HOLE

'When I was working at the Empire before I met Alfred I stayed with Mrs Kopeck at her boarding house. She only took in theatricals. It seems a long time ago now when nobody gave a second thought to another war coming along. One year I was there during the panto-mime season and one of the chorus of one on at the time, a pretty red-head called Maggie, brought the whole cast back to Mrs Kopeck's after the last show on a Saturday. Mrs Kopeck cooked this toad for everyone and used up every egg she had in her pantry. Since then I must have cooked it hundreds of times for the lads from Coltishall and Swanton Morley. John 'W' [U.S.A.A.F., stationed at Hethel] and three of his crew were very suspicious when I told them what they were having for supper one night. They used to ask for it after that though. This is a very English dish and unheard of in America. I wrote the recipe out for John 'W' to send home.'

CHILDREN HARVEST
A GIANT CABBAGE!

INGREDIENTS

3oz flour

2 fresh eggs (dried if necessary)

1/2 a teaspoon of mustard

1/2 a pint of milk

1 teaspoon of salt

1/2 a teaspoon of baking powder

Serves four.

Add flour, baking powder and salt to mixing bowl, mix well. Add mustard and eggs mixing slowly and adding the milk as you go until you have a smooth batter. Leave to stand for at least half an hour. Fry sausages until just brown all over, it will not taste half as good if care is not taken to see that they are. Grease shallow Yorkshire pudding tin of adequate size, large enough to be half filled by mixture, and heat in a hot oven for about ten minutes. Beat batter until just frothy. Pour into heated tin. Evenly place sausages in mixture. Bake for thirty minutes or so until it has risen and turned golden.

For special occasions an ounce of grated cheese may be added to the mixture just before it is poured into the tin and another ounce sprinkled over the top before baking.

Serve at any time as a meal in itself with bitter beer, or for a main meal with vegetables.

'I must say I like mine with a good stout, builds you up for anything does that.'

TOMATO AND BEAN SOUP

From a diary entry, 1943

'Some of the *Eight-balls were in the Standard at Dereham one Thursday night and they were talking about some of the food they used to have at home. I asked them over for a meal at the weekend or whenever they were free which they said was not often. They said that they liked chilli and beans. As I don't quite know how to cook that I cooked them tomato and bean soup. A recipe I was given by Dorothy Gallant, who I worked with for a time at the Star in Gravesend. She used to give me recipes her uncle Harry gave her. He was a steward on the White Star Line. He had applied for a job on the Titanic but was put on the sister ship, the Olympic I think, instead, lucky for him.'

INGREDIENTS

1lb tomatoes

1 good sized onion

2 medium sized potatoes

3 sticks of celery if available

4oz peas (if dried soak overnight)

1 tin of baked beans

1/2 pint of water

1 crushed clove

1/4 pint of milk

Serves four. Increase quantities as required.

Chop tomatoes and vegetables small, finely chop onion. Bring to the boil and simmer. When potato pieces are tender add baked beans and peas. Push through sieve. Soup can then be reheated when required, adding milk and stirring all the time until thick and hot. Serve with plenty of fresh bread. For a main meal it can be served with dumplings.

---

* USAAF 8th Bomber Group

VEGETABLE HOB POT

Serves 14 reduce ingredients as necessary for less.

'Frankie 'T' says that this is the kind of meal his aunt Kate used to make when he used to stay with her in Brixton, she was a widow with not much money and could not afford much meat, another type of rationing. His cousins didn't like it but Frankie did, so he got more. I cooked this for his birthday one Saturday in 1940 just before he was posted to Kent. There were 14 of us, Frankie, eight other aircrew from his airfield, Mavis, Jack, George's brother Will who was on a 48hr pass, Jock, Emily and Arthur. George provided a crate of brown ale and I had some whisky in the cupboard. I know there is no meat in this but nobody seemed to worry and it all went. Albert had to make do with some fish that Jock brought for him.'

INGREDIENTS

1lb carrots

1lb cooked haricot beans

1lb onions

1lb potatoes

1 cauliflower

1 1/2lbs tomatoes

1lb cooked macaroni

2 pints of bone stock

4oz margarine

Pepper and salt

Slice onions. Cut peeled potatoes and carrots into small pieces. Place cauliflower into salted water to clean, then pull to pieces and slice the stalk and leaves closest to centre. Place all vegetables into a large casserole dish with margarine. Sprinkle over half a teaspoon of salt and add the two pints of stock. After bringing to boil, simmer slowly for forty minutes, after the first twenty minutes add tomatoes and the cooked haricot beans. The cooked and heated macaroni is to be added just before serving. Add pepper to taste just before taking to table. Serve with thick fresh bread and brown ale.

REMEMBERING THE POW'S

FURTHER STUDY

My websites have links that will lead to many others I have found and are invaluable in different ways:

- www.nicholaswebley.freewebspace.com (my own site with many links which are updated on a regular basis)
- www.atasteofwartimebritain.freewebspace.com

These websites are, at time of writing, the very best I have seen. Most are regularly maintained and invaluable to any readers desiring to learn more about the Second World War:

- www.nara.gov
- www.wargunner.co.uk
- www.ww2poster.co.uk (The Midnight Watch site)
- www.homesweethomefront.co.uk
- www.bbc.co.uk
- www.457thbombgroup.org
- www.hbo.com/band/landing/currahee.html
- www.whispersfromwalmington.com – one of the great Websites of the world
- www.ibiscom.com
- www.activehistory.co.uk
- www.sentimentaljourney.co.uk
- www.web.ukonline.co.uk/lait/site/index.htm
- www.atschool.eduweb.co.uk/chatback/english/memories/memories. html
- www.wartime-memories.fsnet.co.uk
- www.thisisguernsey.com

AVIATION HISTORY

- www.zenadsl5657.zen.co.uk/spitfire/capel.htm
- www.raf.mod.uk/bob1940/bobhome.html
- www.bbmf.co.uk/index.html
- www.iwm.org.uk/duxford/battofbrit.htm
- www.rafmuseum.org.uk/home.cfm
- www.kbobm.org
- www.flight-history.com

HERE YOU ARE! DON'T LOSE IT AGAIN

OTHER THOROGOOD TITLES

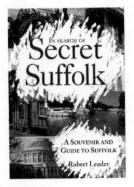

IN SEARCH OF SECRET SUFFOLK

Robert Leader

£9.99 paperback, published in 2004

A book of discovery which explores the heritage and landscape of Suffolk. Uniquely, it follows the course of each of Suffolk's rivers and looks at the towns, villages, stately homes and churches that grew up in their valleys. Robert Leader also charts the medieval history and tradition of the once great abbeys, castles and guildhalls.

IN WAR AND PEACE – THE LIFE AND TIMES OF DAPHNE PEARSON GC

An autobiography

£17.99 cased, published in 2002

Daphne Pearson, born in 1911, was the first woman to be given the George Cross, it was awarded for acts of courage in circumstances of extreme danger. This is the inspiring story of a very courageous and remarkable woman.

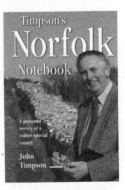

TIMPSON'S NORFOLK NOTEBOOK

John Timpson

£9.99 paperback, published in 2002

A collection of renowned writer and broadcaster John Timpson's best writing about Norfolk, its ancient and subtle landscape, places with strange tales to tell, remarkable and eccentric people and old legends and traditions.

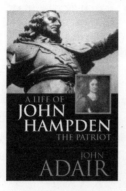

A LIFE OF JOHN HAMPDEN
– THE PATRIOT

John Adair

£12.99 paperback, published in 2003

John Hampden, statesman and soldier, was a cousin to Oliver Cromwell and, had he not met an untimely death at the Battle of Chalgrove during the Civil World War in 1643, he might well have achieved similar fame in English history, both as a soldier and parliamentarian. This classic study of a great man has been out of print for some years and is now published in paperback for the first time.

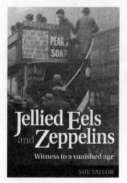

JELLIED EELS AND ZEPPELINS

Sue Taylor

£8.99 paperback, published in 2003

As every year goes by, the number of people able to give a first hand account of day-to-day life in the early part of the last century naturally diminishes. The small but telling detail disappears. Ethel May Elvin was born in 1906; she recalls her father's account of standing sentry at Queen Victoria's funeral, the privations and small pleasures of a working class Edwardian childhood, growing up through the First World War and surviving the Second. Anyone intrigued by the small events of history, how the majority actually lived day-to-day, will find this a unique and fascinating book.

CONFESSIONS OF A COUNTRY BOY

Keith Skipper

£8.99 paperback, published in 2002

Memories of a Norfolk childhood fifty years ago: this is broadcaster and humorist Keith Skipper in his richest vein, sharp and witty, occasionally disrespectful, always affectionate. As he says himself 'Distance may lend enchantment, but my country childhood has inspired much more than rampant nostalgia. I relish every chance to extol the virtues of a golden age when... life was quieter, slower, simpler...'

'He delights our days and does so much for Norfolk.'
Malcolm Bradbury

BETTY'S WARTIME DIARY – 1939-1945

Edited by Nicholas Webley

£9.99 paperback, published in 2002

The Second World War diary of a Norfolk seamstress. Here, the great events of those years are viewed from the country: privation relieved by poaching, upheaval as thousands of bright young US servicemen 'invade' East Anglia, quiet heroes and small -time rural villains. Funny, touching and unaffectedly vivid.

'Makes unique reading... I am finding it fascinating.'
David Croft, co-writer and producer of BBC's hit comedy series 'Dad's Army'